SUMAN KALYANPUR

51 SONGS' SARGAM

A rare collection of Songs Lyrics and its Sargam
sung by Suman Kalyanpur
having fresh clean natural waterfall like voice

SUMAN KALYANPUR

Notation writer: Vinod Kumar

Notion Press

Vinod Kumar

NOTION PRESS

India. Singapore. Malaysia.

ISBN xxx-x-xxxxx-xx-x

DEDICATION

This book is dedicated to my Parents.

-Vinod Kumar

CONTENTS

SINGER SUMAN KALYANPUR BIOGRAPHY

सुमन कल्याणपुर

Birth- 28 January 1937

Age- 85 Years (in Jan 2022)

Parents- Sita Hemmadi, Shankar Rao Hemmadi

Suman Kalyanpur (born as Suman Hemmadi; 28 January 1937) is an Indian playback singer, one of the best-known and most respected playback singers in India.

Her voice was often mistaken to be that of Lata Mangeshkar. Suman Kalyanpur's career started in 1954 and was very popular singer in the 1960s and 1970s. She recorded songs for movies in several languages besides Hindi, Marathi, Assamese, Gujarati, Kannada, Maithili, Bhojpuri, Rajasthani, Bengali, Odia and Punjabi. She is considered among the popular singers of her prime time and golden era of Hindi film music.

Early life

Suman Kalyanpur was born as Suman Hemmadi on 28 January 1937 in Dhaka (now in Bangladesh). Suman Kalyanpur's father

Shankar Rao Hemmadi hailed from a Saraswat Brahmin family belonging to Mangalore. Hemmadi is a village in Kundapur Taluk of Udupi District, Karnataka. He served on a top post in the Central Bank of India and was posted to Dhaka for a very long period. Apart from father and mother Seeta Hemmadi, there were 5 daughters and one son in the family with Suman being the eldest among her siblings. In 1943, her family moved to Mumbai, where she started learning music.

Suman had always been interested in painting and music. After completing schooling from Mumbai's famed St. Columba High School, she got admission in the prestigious Sir J. J. School of Arts for further studies in painting. Simultaneously, she started learning classical vocal from Pune's Prabhat Films' music director and a close family friend, Pandit Keshav Rao Bhole. According to Suman, initially singing was just hobby to her but gradually her interest in music increased and she started learning it professionally from Ustad Khan, Abdul Rehman Khan and Guruji Master Navrang. Suman's younger sister Shyama Hemmady was also a singer.

Married life

Suman Hemmady married a Mumbai-based businessman Ramanand Kalyanpur in the 1958 and thus, became Suman Kalyanpur from Suman Hemmady. He accompanied her for every recording session after her marriage. She has a daughter named Charul Agni who is settled in the United States after marriage. Her grand daughter Aaishanni Agny returned to India and opened an NGO in Mumbai in her grand mother's name.

Career

According to Suman, "Everybody at home had an inclination towards arts and music but public performances were strictly prohibited. Still, I could not say 'no' to an offer to sing for the All India Radio in 1952. This was my first public performance after which I got a chance to sing for the Marathi film Shukrachi Chandni released in the year 1953. At that time, Sheikh Mukhtar was making the film 'Mangu' whose composer was Mohammed Shafi. Sheikh Mukhtar was so impressed with my ''Shukrachi Chandni'' songs, that he got me to sing 3 songs for the film 'Mangu'. However, due to some unknown reasons, later O. P. Nayyar replaced Mohammed Shafi and only one of my three songs, a lullaby "Koi Pukare Dheere Se Tujhe" was retained in the film. Thus, I entered Hindi cinema with the 1954 release "Mangu". Immediately, after the film "'Mangu'", Suman sang 5 songs under the baton of composer Naushad for the film Darwaza (1954), which was produced by Ismat Chugtai and directed by Shahid Lateef. Since ''Darwaza'' released first, it is generally believed to be Suman Kalyanpur's first Hindi film. In the same year (1954), Suman sang the film version of O.P.Nayyar's hit ensemble song "Mohabbat Kar Lo Ji Bhar Lo Aji Kisne Roka Hai" with Mohammed Rafi and Geeta Dutt for the film Aar Paar. According to Suman, she had a couple of solo lines to sing and her services were used, more, as a chorus singer in this song. This proved to be the only song she ever sang for O. P. Nayyar.

Suman Kalyanpur's first film song was a duet with Talat Mahmood in Darwaza (1954). Talat Mahmood heard Kalyanpur singing in a musical concert and was highly impressed by her singing. A rank newcomer, her career hit the big league when Talat agreed to sing the duet with her, making the film industry sit up and take notice of her.

She sang for the movie, Mangu (1954), Koi Pukare Dheere Se Tujhe. Kalyanpur provided playback singing for Miyan Bibi Razi

(1960), Baat Ek Raat Ki (1962), Dil Ek Mandir (1963), Dil Hi To Hai (1963), Shagoon (1964), Jahan Ara (1964), Sanjh Aur Savera (1964), Noor Jehan (1967), Saathi (1968) and Pakeezah (1971). She sang for composers Shankar Jaikishan, Roshan, Madan Mohan, S. D. Burman, N Datta, Hemant Kumar, Chitragupta, Naushad, S. N. Tripathi, Ghulam Mohammed, Kalyanji Anandji and Laxmikant–Pyarelal singing the most songs for the first two in the list. She has sung over 740 movie and non-movie songs. She sang over 140 duets with Rafi in the 1960s.

Suman's first song in Marathi was the super-hit "Bhaatuklichaa Khel Maandila" for Vasant Prabhu, for the film Pasant Aahe Mulgi. After that she never looked back for over 20 years. Putra Vhawa Aisaa, Ekti, Manini and Annapoorna were but a few of her memorable films. But even outside films, her hits are legion and include over 50 timeless gems of Marathi films, bhavgeet and bhaktigeet.

She recorded some popular duets with male singers Mohammed Rafi, Manna Dey, Mukesh, Talat Mahmood, and Hemant Kumar. Some of her memorable duets with Rafi are "Aajkal Tere Mere Pyaar Ke Charche", "Na Na Karte Pyaar", "Tumse O Hasina", "Rahen Na Rahen Hum", "Parbaton Ke Pedon Par Shaam Ka Basera He", "Ajahu na Aye Balama", "Tumane Pukara Aur Hum Chale Aye", "Bad Muddat Ke Yeh Ghadi Ayee", "Mujhe Yeh Bhool Na", "Dil Ne Phir Yaad Kiya", "Tujhko Dilbari Ki Kasam" and "Chand Takata Hai Idhar". With Manna Dey, she sang the popular duet "Na Jane Kahan Ham The" under the music direction of Dattaram. With Mukesh she has sung many popular duets like `Yeh Kisne Geet Chheda', "Akhiyon ka noor hai tu", "Mera Pyar Bhi Tu Hai", "Dil Ne Phir Yaad Kiya", "Shama Se Koi Kehde", etc.

Kalyanpur also recorded some memorable songs with a classical base, including "Manamohan Man Mein Ho Tumhi", "Mere Sang Ga Gunguna" and "Gir Gayi Re More Mathe Ki Bindiya".

Similarity of voice with Lata Mangeshkar

Suman Kalyanpur's voice was very similar to the singer, Lata Mangeshkar and some times people can not differ her voice with Lata's voice and think of Lata's song.

When Lata was not available for recording, or if the producers could not afford her rate of per song, the song used to be sung by Suman Kalyanpur. During the similar period, Lata had refused to sing with Rafi over royalty issues and those songs of Md. Rafi were recorded with Suman Kalyanpur and a great voice came in front of the music listeners. She sang over 140 duets with Rafi in this period.

Notable songs

Hindi songs

- "Sathi Mere Sathi" (Veerana)
- "Na Tum Hamen Jano" (Baat Ek Raat Ki)
- "Chhodo, Chhodo Mori Baiyann" (Miya Biwi Razi)
- "Dil Gham Se Jal Raha" (Shama)
- "Yun Hi Dil Ne Chaha Tha" (Dil Hi To Hai)
- "Bujha Diye Hain" (Shagoon)
- "Mere Sang Ga" (Janwar)
- "Mere Mehboob Na Ja" (Noor Mahal)
- "Tum Agar Aa Sako To"' and
- "Zindagi Doob Gai Dard Ke Toofano Mein" (Ek Sal Pehle)
- "Zindagi imtehan leti hai " (Naseeb)
- "Jo Ham Pe Guzarti Hai" (Mohabbat Isko Kehten Hain)

- "Sharabi Sharabi Yeh Sawan Ka Mausam" (Noor Jehan)
- "Behena Ne Bhai Ki Kalai Main" (Resham Ki Dori), for which she was nominated for the Filmfare Best Female Playback Award in 1975.
- "Dil Ek Mandir Hai" (Dil Ek Mandir)
- "Aajkal Tere Mere Pyaar Ke Charche" from Brahmachari, which was one of her most famous songs, is usually thought to be sung by Lata Mangeshkar but it was in fact sung by her. (The confusion results from the fact that the quality of her voice is similar to Lata Mangeshkar's at times).
- "Aansoo ki ek boond hoon main" (Ek Paheli)
- "Mera Pyar Bhi Tu Hai Yeh Bahar Bhi Tu Hai" (Saathi)
- "Na Na Karte Pyar" (Jab Jab Phool Khile)
- "Zindagi zulm sahi" (shagun)

Marathi songs

- "Rimjhhim Jharati Shrāwan Dhara"
- "Shabda Shabda Japun Thhewa"
- "Re Kshanichya Sangateene Mi Ashi Bharawale"
- "Keshava Madhava Tuzya Namat Re Godawa"
- "Omkar Pradhan Roop Ganeshache"
- "Jethe Sagara Dharanee Milate"
- "Bhaktichya Phulancha Goad To Suwas"
- "Navika Re Vara Vahe Re"
- "Ketakichya Banee Tethe Nachala Ga Mor"
- "Yaa Laadkya Mulino".
- "Samadhi Gheun jayee dnyandev".
- "Mrudul Karani Chhedit Tara".
- "Savalya Vitthala Tujhya Dari Aale".
- "Saang kadhi kalnar tula bhav majhya manat la"
- "Nimbonichya zada mage"

Bengali songs

- "Ronger Basore"
- "Ei Chadro Mollikate"
- "Durashar Baluchare"
- "Mone Karo Aami Nei"
- "Sudhu Swapno Niye"
- "Kande Keno Mon"
- "Tomar Aakash Theke"
- "Badoler Madol Baje Guruguru"
- "Aamar Swapno Dekhar Duti Nayon"
- "Aakash Ajana Tobu"
- "Payer Chinho Niye"
- "Dulchere Mon"
- "Byatha Hoye Keno Phire Ele Bondhua"
- "Bhabis Ne Re Kandhchi Bosey"
- "Ekhane Okhane Jekhane Sekhane"
- "Dure theko na aaro aaro kache eso"

Kannada songs

- "Odanadi Bekendu"
- "Hani Hani Heeri Thani Hareya"
- "Thallana Nooru bage"

Awards

1. Received three times the prestigious "Sur Sringar Samsad" award for the best classical song in a Hindi movie.
2. Lata Mangeshkar Award 2009 by the Maharashtra government
3. Ga Di Ma Award by Ga Di Ma Pratishthan

Vinod Kumar

PREFACE

My hearty greetings and Namaste to Readers. I have written 51 Songs' Sargam books of Mukesh-1,2, Kishor-1,2, Lata, Asha, Manna dey, Yesudas, Kumar Shanu, Rafi-1,2,3,4 and SD Burman's composed song book in Hindi Language and translated many books in English SARGAM and Western CDEFG. Bhajan Swarlipi 1,2,3 and one Gazal Sargam book is also published in Hindi, English and Western notes. All these books are available online. Now I have translated the Suman Kalyanpur ke 51 Geeton ki Sargam book in English as Suman Kalyanpur 51 Songs' Sargam. It is in English SRGM notes, so that music lovers can play and sing songs and get enjoyed. A person having basic knowledge of music can play the songs on any instrument.

Mostly song's notations are written in original scale but somewhere you have to transpose +1 or − 1 or ±2 to get original scale. Sa taken is also mentioned in each song's detail. Person who knows western notations can understand as given below:

.नी	.नी	सा	रे॒	रे	ग॒	ग	म
.$\underline{N}$	.N	S	$\underline{R}$	R	$\underline{G}$	G	M
.B^b	.B	C	D^b	D	E^b	E	F
.$A^{\#}$	.B	C	$C^{\#}$	D	$D^{\#}$	E	F

मे	प	ध॒	ध	नी॒	नी	सां	रें॒
M*	P	$\underline{D}$	D	$\underline{N}$	N	S'	$\underline{R}'$
G^b	G	A^b	A	B^b	B	C'	$D^{b\prime}$
$F^{\#}$	G	$G^{\#}$	A	$A^{\#}$	B	C'	$C^{\#\prime}$

In this book some symbols are given as (G-) it means you have to play G for two beats duration or matra similarly you have to play for the beats for more number of – if there are more dashes. When two notes are written adjacending to each other it means you have to play the notes in one beat or matra as MP mapa is played in one beat.

Notations at the beginning of the song are prelude and notations in the middle of the song are interlude. These notations are written by me by my experience. Hope readers shall understand, like and enjoy it.

One has to practice sargam daily and its palte also so that one can become expert in playing difficult notes sequence. People can enjoy your playing instruments and then only your success will be counted. Care has been taken to provide accuracy still there is no liability of correctness and accuracy of notes and writer, printer, publisher and editor is not respoinsible for any error or ommissions or mistakes. If any mistake is found kindly inform.

For purchasing the books in India, one can visit notionpress.com or flipkart.com and amazon.in. Kindly review my books at amazon and flipkart and give proper stars after purchasing my books from the above sites. For any query, email to me.

- Vinod Kumar (vinod66vk@gmail.com)

SARGAM

SARGAM swars/sound are derived from voice of animals and birds. C scale is as follows:-

Note Name	Swar	स्वर नाम	Swar full name	स्वर का पूरा नाम हिंदी में	यह स्वर किस पशु पछी की आवाज से लिया गया है.
C=	Sa=	सा	Shadaj	षडज	Peacock/ मोर की आवाज़
D=	Re=	रे	Rishabh	रिषभ	Papiha /पपीहा की आवाज़
E=	Ga=	ग	Gandhar	गन्धार	Goat/ बकरा की आवाज़
F=	Ma=	म	Madhyam	मध्यम	Crane/ बगुला की आवाज़
G=	Pa=	प	Pancham	पंचम	Koccoo/Koyal/ कोयल की आवाज़
A=	Dha=	ध	Dhaiwat	धैवत	Frog/ दादुर या मेंढक की आवाज़
B=	Ni=	नी	Nishad	निषाद	Elephant हाथी की आवाज़
C'=	Sa'=	सां	(Higher Sa)		

C#=R̲e=रॆ (रे कोमल), D#=G̲a=ग॒ (ग कोमल), F#=Ma*=मे (म तीव्र), G#=D̲ha=ध॒ (ध कोमल), A#=N̲i=नी॒ (नी कोमल)

We can write as S R̲ R G̲ G M M* P D̲ D N̲ N S'

All notes underlined are called Komal Swar as Komal Re Komal Ga Komal Dha Komal Ni. One note Ma* is called Tivra Ma Sequence of the notes are-

S	R̲	R	G̲	G	M	M*
सा	रॆ	रे	ग॒	ग	म	मे
C	D^b	D	E^b	E	F	G^b
C	$C^\#$	D	$D^\#$	E	F	$F^\#$

P	D̲	D	N̲	N	S'
प	ध॒	ध	नी॒	नी	सां
G	A^b	A	B^b	B	C'
G	$G^\#$	A	$A^\#$	B	C'

Sa and Pa are Shudha Swar they do not have any Komal or Tivra. They are fixed notes as per North Indian music tradition.

OCTAVE

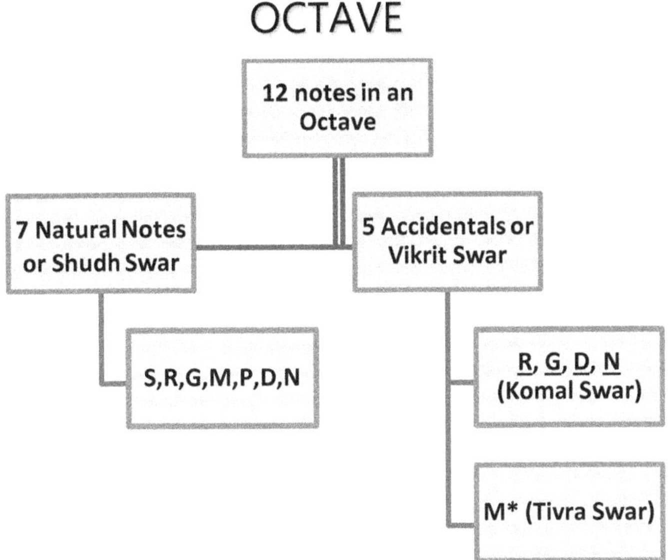

Sequence of the notes on any instrument are:

.D .D .N .N S R R G G M M* P D D N N S' R' R' G' G'

C# Scale is given as under:

S R G M P D N S'

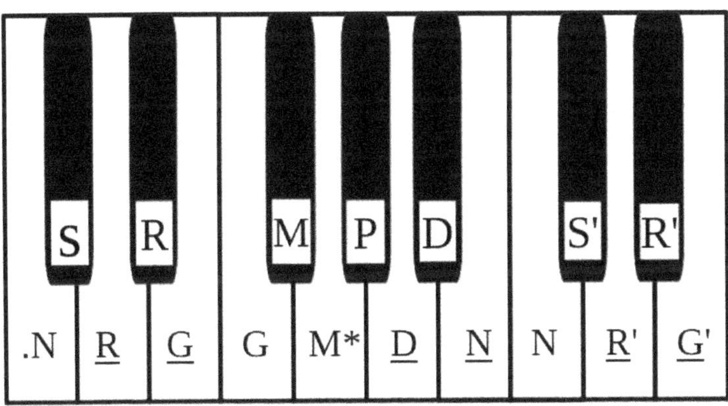

1.   ANKHIYON KA NOOR HAI TU

Film: Jauhar Mahmood in Goa (1965)   Music: Kalyanji Anandji
Lyrics: Qamar Jalalabadi   Singer: Mukesh, Suman K.
Taal: Kaharwa   Chord: M<u>D</u>S'   S=D

ankhiyon ka nur hai tu, ankhiyon se dur hai tu
fir bhi pukaare chale jaayenge, tu aye na aye
fir bhi pukaare chale jaayenge

dil men payaam tera lab pe hai naam tera
ho ke diwaane tere pyaar men lo aye ji aye
ho ke diwaane tere pyaar men

o mere hamaraaz kahaan hai, mujh ko de awaaz kahaan hai
pyaar ki ankhon se tum dekho, <u>ishq wahin hai husn jahaan hai</u> -2
chhup chhup ke anewaale, dil ko jalaane waale
chupake se aa ja mere saamne
tu aja re a ja, chupake se a ja mere saamne

isalie aya hun main chhupake, dekh ke hamako duniya jale na
pyaar ki mahafil kitani anokhi, <u>nur hai lekin dip jale na</u>-2
yaadon ke daag le ke, dil ke chiraag le ke
kab se khada hun tere saamne
tu maane na maane kab se khada hun tere saamne

ANKHIYON KA NOOR HAI TU

dha	ge	n	ti	n	ke	dhi	n	dha	ge	n	ti	n	ke	dhi	n
1	2	3	4	5	6	7	8	1	2	3	4	5	6	7	8
		S	R	-	R	M	M	M	P	-	D	D	-	D	-
		an	khi	-	yon	-	ka	nu	-	-	r	hai	-	tu	-
-	-	P	D	-	P	-	M	M	P	-	D	D	-	D	-
-	-	an	khi	-	yon	-	se	du	-	-	r	hai	-	tu	-
-	-	P	D	-	P	-	M	M	P	P	D	-	P	P	-
-	-	fi	r	-	bhi	-	pu	ka	-	re	-	-	ch	le	-
M	-	-	M	M	-	M	-	M	P	P	N	N	-	D	-
ja	-	-	yen	ge	-	tu	-	aa	-	ye	n	aa	-	ye	-
-	-	P	D	-	P	-	M	M	P	P	D	-	P	P	-
-	-	fi	r	-	bhi	-	pu	ka	-	re	-	-	ch	le	-
M	-	-	M	M	-	-	-	D	P	D	-	P	M	M	-
ja	-	-	yen	ge	-	-	-	-	-	-	-	-	-	-	-
-	-	S	R	-	R	M	M	M	P	-	-	D	D	D	-
-	-	di	l	-	me	-	p	ya	-	-	-	m	te	ra	-
-	-	D	D	-	P	M	-	M	P	-	-	D	D	D	-
-	-	l	b	-	pe	hai	-	na	-	-	-	m	te	ra	-
-	-	D	-	-	P	-	M	M	P	P	D	-	P	-	M
-	-	ho	-	-	ke	-	di	va	-	ne	-	-	te	-	re
M	-	-	M	M	-	M	-	M	P	P	N	N	-	D	-
pya	-	-	r	me	-	lo	-	aa	-	ye	ji	aa	-	ye	-
-	-	D	-	-	P	-	M	M	P	P	D	-	P	-	M
-	-	ho	-	-	ke	-	di	va	-	ne	-	-	te	-	re

```
M   -   -   M | M   -         |              |
pya -   -   r | me  -         |              |
```

interlude:

M' N S' R'- M'G'R'M'- S'N ND DN- M'G'R'M'- S'N ND DN-
R'S' S'N ND DN-D PD-P M
M- MG- GR- RS-
M'—G'M'P'S'R'—NS'R'DN
N DP PM P M (MDS')

			S'	-		-	N	-	-	N	-	-	-	N	S'	R'	-
			o	-		-	me	-	-	re	-	-	-	hm	-	-	-
-	-	S'	-		-	N	-	N	N	-	-	-	N	-	-	-
-	-	ra	-		-	z	-	k	ha	-	-	-	hai	-	-	-
-	-	S'	N		-	N	-	-	N	-	-	-	PD	ᴾD	-	-
-	-	mu	jh		-	ko	-	-	de	-	-	-	aa-	-	-	-
-	-	D	P		-	P	-	M	M	-	-	-	M	-	-	-
-	-	va	-		-	z	-	k	ha	-	-	-	hai	-	-	-
-	-	S'	-		-	N	-	N	N	-	-	-	N	S'	R'	-
-	-	pya	-		-	r	-	ki	aan	-	-	-	khon	-	-	-
-	-	S'	-		-	N	-	N	N	-	-	-	N	-	-	-
-	-	se	-		-	tu	-	m	de	-	-	-	kho	-	-	-
-	-	S'	-		-	N	-	D	D	-	-	-	PD	ᴾD	-	-
-	-	i	-	sh	q	-	v	hin	-	-	-	hai-	-	-	-
-	-	N	D		-	P	-	M	M	-	-	-	M	-	M	P
-	-	hu	s		-	n	-	j	ha	-	-	-	hai	-	-	-
D	-	D	-		-	N	-	S'	N	-	-	-	M	G	-	-
-	-	i	-	sh	k	-	v	hin	-	-	-	hai	-	-	-

-	-	D	D	-	P	-	M	M	-	-	-	M	-	-	-
-	-	hu	s	-	n	-	j	ha	-	-	-	hai	-	-	-
-	-	S	-	R	-	M	-	M	-	P	D	D	-	D	-
-	-	chhu	p	chhu	p	ke	-	aa	-	ne	-	va	-	le	-
-	-	P	D	-	P	-	M	M	-	P	D	D	-	D	-
-	-	di	l	-	ko	-	j	la	-	ne	-	va	-	le	-
-	-	P	D	P	-	M	-	M	-	P	D	-	P	P	-
-	-	chu	p	ke	-	se	-	aa	-	ja	-	-	me	re	-
M	-	-	M	M	-	-	M	M	P	P	N	N	-	D	-
sa	-	-	m	ne	-	-	tu	aa	-	ja	re	aa	-	ja	-
-	-	P	D	P	M	M	-	M	P	P	D	-	P	-	P
-	-	chu	p	ke	-	se	-	aa	-	ja	-	-	me	-	re
M	-	-	M	M	-	-	-	D	P	D	-	P	M	M	-
sa	-	-	m	ne	-	-	-	-	-	-	-	-	-	-	-
-	-	S	R	-	M	-	M	M	P	-	-	D	D	D	-
-	-	di	l	-	me	-	p	ya	-	-	-	m	te	ra	-
-	-	D	D	-	P	M	-	M	P	-	-	D	D	D	-
-	-	l	b	-	pe	hai	-	na	-	-	-	m	te	ra	-
-	-	D	-	-	P	-	M	M	P	P	D	-	P	-	M
-	-	ho	-	-	ke	-	di	va	-	ne	-	-	te	-	re
M	-	-	M	M	-	M	-	M	P	P	N	N	-	D	-
pya	-	-	r	me	-	lo	-	aa	-	ye	ji	aa	-	ye	-
-	-	P	D	-	P	-	M	M	P	P	D	-	P	P	-
-	-	ho	-	-	ke	-	di	va	-	ne	-	-	te	re	-

M - - M | M -
pya - - r | me -

S'NNN NNS'R' S' N   NNN   S'N N D P D   PPD   PM M
islie   aaya hu main chhupke,dekh ke hmko- duniya jle na

S'N N N NS'R' S'NN   NNN S'N D   DPD ND PM M
pyar ki mhfil-   kitni anokhi, nur hai lekin dip jle   na
music: M P D-

DN S' N MGD   DP MM M
nur hai lekin-- dip jle   na

SR   M MPD D D PD P MMPD D D
yado ke da-g le ke, dil ke chira-g le ke

PD P MM PD PM MMM
kb se khda hu- tere samne

M MP   N ND   PD P MM PD PM MMM   DPD- PMM-
tu mane na mane kb se khda hu-tere samne (music)

		S	R		R	M	M	M	P		D	D		D	
		an	khi	-	yon	-	ka	nu	-	-	r	hai	-	tu	-
-	-	P	D	-	P	-	M	M	P	-	D	D	-	D	-
-	-	an	khi	-	yon	-	se	du	-	-	r	hai	-	tu	-
-	-	P	D	-	P	-	M	M	P	P	D	-	P	P	-
-	-	fi	r	-	bhi	-	pu	ka	-	re	-	-	ch	le	-
M	-	-	M	M	-	M	-	M	P	P	N	N	-	D	-
ja	-	-	yen	ge	-	tu	-	aa	-	ye	n	aa	-	ye	-
-	-	P	D	-	P	-	M	M	P	P	D	-	P	P	-
-	-	fi	r	-	bhi	-	pu	ka	-	re	-	-	ch	le	-

M	-	-	M	M	-	-	-	
ja	-	-	yen	ge	-	-	-	

2.   AGAR TERI JALWANUMAI NA HOTI

Film: Beti Bete (1964)
Lyrics: Hasrat Jaipuri
Taal: Kaharwa

Music: Shanker Jaikishan
Singer: Md. Rafi, Suman K.
Chord: RPN   S=D

Rafi: agar teri jalwa numai na hoti,
khuda ki kasam ye khudayi na hoti

Suman:agar aankh tumse milayi na hoti
meri zindagi muskurayi na hoti

Rafi: baharo ka mausam na hota suhana -2
tere dam kadam se hua aashikana -2
nazaaro me ye dil rubai na hoti
khuda ki kasam ye khudayi na hoti
agar aankh tumse milayi na hoti
meri jindagi muskurayi na hoti

Suman:tere pyar ne mujh par ahsaan kiya hai -2
mere dil liya hai mujhe dil diya hai -2
agar tune ulfat nibhayi na hoti
meri zindagi muskurayi na hoti
agar teri jalwa numai na hoti
khuda ki kasam ye khudayi na hoti

Rafi: agar noor tera na aata jaha me -2
to rakha hi kaya tha zamii aasma me -2
ke malik ne dunia banayi na hoti
khuda ki kasam ye khudayi na hoti

agar aankh tumse milayi na hoti, meri zindagi muskurayi na hoti
agar teri jalwa numai na hoti, khuda ki kasam ye khudayi na hoti.

AGAR TERI JALWANUMAI NA HOTI

dha	ge	n	ti	n	ke	dhi	n	dha	ge	n	ti	n	ke	dhi	n
1	2	3	4	5	6	7	8	1	2	3	4	5	6	7	8

prelude:
PN P'-- M*'-- NP G'—R'— G'R'G'R' G'R'G'R'
DPDP DNDP DPDP DNDP
PM*GR PNDP P-

dha	ge	n	ti	n	ke	dhi	n	dha	ge	n	ti	n	ke	dhi	n
		R	R	N	D	-	P	P	-	-	-	P	-	-	-
		a	g	r	te	-	ri	j	l	-	-	va	-	-	-
-	-	S'	N	-	D	-	P	D	-	-	-	D	-	-	-
-	-	nu	ma	-	ii	-	n	ho	-	-	-	ti	-	-	-
-	-	R'	R'	-	S'	-	N	S'	-	-	-	N	-	-	P
-	-	khu	da	-	ki	-	k	sm	-	-	-	ye	-	-	khu
N	-	-	-	D	-	-	P	P	-	-	-	P	-	-	-
da	-	-	-	yi	-	-	n	ho	-	-	-	ti	-	-	-
-	-	R	R	N	D	-	P	P	-	-	-	P	-	-	-
-	-	a	g	r	aan	-	kh	tum	-	-	-	se	-	-	-
-	-	S'	N	-	D	-	P	D	-	-	-	D	-	-	-
-	-	mi	la	-	ii	-	n	ho	-	-	-	ti	-	-	-
-	-	R'	R'	-	S'	-	N	S'	-	-	-	N	-	-	P
-	-	me	ri	-	zin	-	d	gi	-	-	-	mu	-	-	sku
N	-	-	-	D	-	-	P	P	-	-	-	P	-	-	-
ra	-	-	-	yi	-	-	n	ho	-	-	-	ti	-	-	-

interlude: 1
S'---- R' N N D P DN N D P P –
S'---- R' N N D P DN N D P P –
G'—P' R'G' S'R' NS' DN
DP ND S'--- NDP--

		R'	R'	-	R'	-	R'	G'	-	-	-	S'	N	D	-
		b	ha	-	ro	-	ka	mau	-	-	-	sm	-	-	-
-	-	S'	S'	-	S'	-	S'	R'	-	-	-	N	D	P	-
-	-	n	ho	-	ta	-	su	ha	-	-	-	na	-	-	-
-	-	G	G	-	G	-	M	P	-	-	-	N	-	-	N
-	-	te	re	-	dm	-	k	dm	-	-	-	se	-	-	hu
S'	-	-	-	N	-	-	D	P	-	-	-	P	N	D	P
aa	-	-	-	aa	-	-	shi	ka	-	-	-	na	-	-	-
-	-	R	R	N	D	-	P	P	-	-	-	P	-	-	-
-	-	n	za	-	ro	-	me	ye	-	-	-	dil	-	-	-
-	-	S'	N	-	D	-	P	D	-	-	-	D	-	-	-
-	-	ru	ba	-	ii	-	n	ho	-	-	-	ti	-	-	-
-	-	R'	R'	-	S'	-	N	S'	-	-	-	N	-	-	P
-	-	khu	da	-	ki	-	k	sm	-	-	-	ye	-	-	khu
N	-	-	-	D	-	-	P	P	-	-	-	P	-	-	-
da	-	-	-	ii	-	-	n	ho	-	-	-	ti	-	-	-

interlude: 2

P'---- M'G' G'-M'-G'-M'-

R'-G'-R'-G'-R'-

NR'M'G'R' N DD P-

N-P-N-P- N-P-P- PDNS'R'--

		R'	R'		R'	-	R'	G'	-	-	-	S'	N	D	-
		te	re	-	pya	-	r	ne	-	-	-	mu	jh	pe	-
-	-	S'	S'	-	S'	-	S'	R'	-	-	-	N	D	P	-
-	-	e	h	-	san	-	ki	ya	-	-	-	hai	-	-	-
-	-	G	G	-	G	-	M	P	-	-	-	N	-	-	N
-	-	me	ra	-	dil	-	li	ya	-	-	-	hai	-	-	mu

S'	-	-	-	N	-	-	D	P	-	-	-	P	N	D	P
jhe	-	-	-	dil	-	-	di	ya	-	-	-	hai	-	-	-
-	-	R	R	N	D	-	P	P	-	-	-	P	-	-	-
-	-	a	g	r	tu	-	ne	ul	-	-	-	f	-	-	t
-	-	S'	N	-	D	-	P	D	-	-	-	D	-	-	-
-	-	ni	bha	-	ii	-	n	ho	-	-	-	ti	-	-	-
-	-	R'	R'	-	S'	-	N	S'	-	-	-	N	-	-	P
-	-	me	ri	-	zin	-	d	gi	-	-	-	mu	-	-	sku
N	-	-	-	D	-	-	P	P	-	-	-	P	-	-	-
ra	-	-	-	yi	-	-	n	ho	-	-	-	ti	-	-	-

3.   AJAHUN NA AAYE BAALMA

Film: Sanjh aur Savera (1964)   Music: Shanker Jaikishan
Lyrics: Hasrat Jaipuri   Singer: Md. Rafi, Suman K.
Taal: Kaharwa   Chord: SGP   S=C#

aa aa aa aa aa
ajahun n ae baalama
saawan bita jaae,
haae re saawan bita jaae

nind bhi ankhiyan dwaar na ae
tose milan ki aas bhi jaae
aayi bahaar khile fulawa,
more sapanen kaun sajaae

chaand ko badara garawa lagaae
aur bhi mora man lalachaae
yaar hasin gale lag ja, aa
yaar hasin gale lag ja mori umr gujarati jaae

Vinod Kumar

AJAHUN NA AAYE BAALMA

dha	ge	n	ti	n	ke	dhi	n	dha	ge	n	ti	n	ke	dhi	n
1	2	3	4	5	6	7	8	1	2	3	4	5	6	7	8

prelude: sarangi: G – M S .D .N S

S----- G S .D .N S

aa .... -2

G M D N S'

aa .... -2

P – D P M G   S G ---- .D .N .N S---

aa .... aa.............aa..................... -2

	NN	-S'	S'	DN	S'	D	P	-	MD	N	D	P	M	G	-
	aj	-hu	n	aa-	-	ye	-	-	ba-	-	l	ma	-	-	-
-	G	-M	P	G	-	S	.N	S	-	-	-	S	D	PM	G
-	sa	-v	n	bi	-	ta	-	ja	-	-	y	ha	ye	re-	-
-	G	-M	P	G	-	S	.N	S	-	-	-	MP	DN	S'	-
-	sa	-v	n	bi	-	ta	-	ja	-	-	y	aa-	--	-	-
-	NN	-S'	S	DN	S'	D	P	-	MD	N	D	P	M	G	-
-	aj	-hu	n	aa-	-	ye	-	-	ba	-	l	ma	-	-	-
-	G	-M	P	G	-	S	.N	S	-	-	-	S	D	PM	G
-	sa	-v	n	bi	-	ta	-	ja	-	-	y	ha	ye	re	-
-	G	-M	P	G	-	S	.N	S	-	-	-	GM	PD	NS'	G'
-	sa	-v	n	bi	-	ta	-	ja	-	-	y	aa-	--	--	-
S'	NN	-S'	S	DN	S'	D	P	-	MD	N	D	P	M	G	-
-	aj	-hu	n	aa-	-	ye	-	-	ba	-	l	ma	-	-	-
-	G	-M	P	G	-	S	.N	S	-	-	-	G	-	DP	M
-	sa	-v	n	bi	-	ta	-	ja	-	-	y	ha	ye	re-	-

-	G̲	-M	P	G̲	-	S	.N	S	-	-	-
-	sa	-v	n	bi	-	ta	-	ja	-	-	y

interlude:

sarangi:- G̲' S' R' N S', G̲'—R' M'—R' G̲' – R' S' R' – N S'

violin:-

P'M'P' M'G̲'M' G̲'R'G̲'-

M'G̲' M'G̲'R'S' G̲'R'S'N

NS'ND̲PMG̲RS

G̲	M	M	D̲	D	N	N	-	S'	S'	N	S'	-	S'	-
nin	d	bhi	a	khi	y	n	-	dwa	r	n	aa	-	ye	-

R'	N	D̲	P	M	G̲	M	G̲	-	G̲	M	M	D̲	D	N	N
-	-	-	-	-	-	-	-	-	nin	d	bhi	a	khi	y	n

-	S'	S'	N	S'	-	S'	-	-	N	N	N	S'	S'	S'	-
-	dwa	r	n	aa	-	ye	-	-	to	se	mi	l	n	ki	-

-	N	S'D̲	P	MG̲	M	-	G̲	-	G̲	M	M	D̲	D	N	N
-	aa	-s bhi		ja	ye	-	-	-	nin	d	bhi	a	khi	y	n

-	S'	S'	N	S'	-	S'	-	-	N	N	N	S'	S'	S'	-
-	dwa	r	n	aa	-	ye	-	-	to	se	mi	l	n	ki	-

-	N	S'D̲	P	MG̲	M	-	G̲	-	G̲'	-R'	-S'	G̲'	-	-R'	-S'
-	aa	s bhi		ja-	ye	-	-	-	aa	-ii	-b	ha	-	-r	-khi

D̲	-	-	NN	S'	-	-	-	-	G̲'	-R'	-S'	G̲'	-	-R'	-S'
le	-	-	ful	va	-	-	-	-	aa	-ii	-b	ha	-	-r	-khi

D̲	-	-	NN	S'	-	-	-	-	M'	-G̲'	-S'	D̲	-	-N	-D̲
le	-	-	ful	va	-	-	-	-	aa	-ii	-b	ha	-	-r	-khi

NS'	R'G̲'	M'	G̲'R'	S'	-	S'	N	-	R'S'	-S'	N	S'	-	-D̲	-P
le-	--	-	ful	va	-	mo	re	-	sp	-ne	-	kau	-	-n	-s

MG P M G |GM DN S' -
ja ye - - |aa- -- - -

- NN -S' S' |DN S' D P | - MD N D |P M G -
- aj -hu n |aa- - ye - | - ba - I |ma - - -
interlude: 2 same

GM   M   DDN S'S' NS'S' R'S'NDPGMG
chand ko bdra grva Igae

NN N   S'S'   NS'   DPMGPMG
aur bhi mora mn   IIchhae

G'R' S'G'R' S'D NN S'
yar   hsiin   gle Ig   ja

DNS'R' G'R' S'G'R' S'D NN S'
aa..   yar   hsiin   gle Ig ja

M'G' S'DN DNS'R'G'M' G'R' S'
yar   hsiin gle   Ig   ja

S'N R'S'S' NS'S'D MGPMG
mori umr   guzrti jae

GMDNS' NNS' S'
aa ...   ajhu n -

4. APNE PIYA KI MAIN TO BANI RE JOGANIYA

Film: Kan Kan me Bhagwan (1963)   Music: Shivram
Lyrics: Bharat Vyas   Singer: Suman K.
Taal: Kaharwa dugun   Chord: M<u>D</u>S'   S=C#

piya charan ki babhoot ramaayi,
preet ki pahni mala
ab kaahe ka darna jag se,
man mein huaa ujala, aaa

apne piya ki main to bani re joganiya
hansi udaaye chaahe saari duniya,
main to bani re joganiya
apne piya ki main to bani re joganiya

saawariya ke rang mein chunariya rangaungi -2
chandrma ka jhumka pahan piya aaungi
jhan jhan baaje mori ho o.. o..
jhan jhan baaje mori jhaanjhariya
main to bani re joganiya

tere liye maine to sharam laaj chhodi re -2
tere sang jodi to jagat sang todi re
tu hai mohan mera, ho, o.. o..
tu hai mohan main teri mohaniya,
main to bani re joganiya

APNE PIYA KI MAIN TO BANI RE JOGANIYA

dhage	nti	nke	dhin	dhage	nti	nke	dhin	dhage	nti	nke	dhin	dhage	nti	nke	dhin
12	34	56	78	12	34	56	78	12	34	56	78	12	34	56	78

S'S' S'S'S' S'   S'M'M' G'M'M' S'M'G' S'   NS'ND   NS'R' S'
piya chrn ki   bhbhut rmaii,   pri-t ki   p h ni- ma--- la

MD   R'R'   R' NS'R'   NS' D   D   D   DNS'   DDNM*M
ab   kahe ka drna   jg   se, mn me huaa- uja-la-,

MDNR'--- S'NS'   NDN GM
aa -----   aa-------aa------
tune:

	MN	N	N	D	D	D	M	M	D	D	D	M	M	M	-
-	N	N	N	N	S'	N	D	D	N	S'	D	N	-	D	M
M	D	D	D	M	M	M	-								

M   M   D   D   N   N   S'   M   M   M   D   D   N   N   S'   -
saan vri ya ke   rn   g   main chu n   ri ya rn   ga   un   gi   -

M   M   D   D   N   N   S'   M   M   M   D   D   N   N   S'   -
chn dr ma ka   jhu   m   ka   p   h   n   pi ya   aa   un   gi   -

-    S' S'S' S'   S'   R'   S'   N   N   -   N   -   N   D   NR' S'
-    jh njh n   ba   je   mo   ri   o   -   o   -   o   -   o   -

-    S' S'S' S'   S'   R'   S'   N   N   -   S'   D   N   -   D   M
-    jh njh n   ba   je   mo   ri   jhan -   jh   ri   ya   -   main to

M   D   D   D   M   M   M   -   -   MN N   N   D   D   D   M
b   ni   re   jo   g   ni   ya   -   -   ap ne pi   ya   ki main to

M   D   D   D   M   M   M   -   -   N   N   N   N   S'   N   D
b   ni   re   jo   g   ni   ya   -   -   hn sii u   da   ye chha he

D N S' D	N - D M	M D D D	M M M -
sa ri du ni	ya - main to	b ni re jo	g ni ya -
- MN N N	D D D M	M D D D	M M M -
- ap ne pi	ya ki main to	b ni re jo	g ni ya -

interlude: play sthayi.

M M D D	N N S' M	M M D -D	N NS' S' -
te re li ye	main ne to sh	r m la -j	chho di- re -
M M D D	N N S' M	M M D -D	N NS' S' -
te re sn g	jo di to j	g t sn g	to di re -

- S' S' S'	S' R' S' N	N - N -	N D NR' S'
- tu hai mo	h n me ra	ho - o -	o - o- -
- S' S' S'	S' R' S' N	N - S' D	N - D M
- tu hai mo	hn main te	ri mo - h ni	yan - main to

M D D M	M M M -	- MN N N	D D D M
b ni re jo	g ni ya -	- ap ne pi	ya ki main to
M D D D	M M M -		
b ni re jo	g ni ya -		

5.   ALLAH KARAM KARNA

Film: Dada (1979)　　　　　　　Music: Usha Khanna
Lyrics: Gauhar Kanpuri　　　　　Singer: Suman K.
Taal: Daadra　　　　　　　　　Chord: M$\underline{D}$R'　S=D

hum sabko nek raah chalana mere allaah
bandon ko buraai se bachana mere allaah
allaah karam karna maula tu reham karna
allaah karam karna maula tu reham karna

ik vaakayaa sunaati hun main apni zubaani
apne badon se maine suni hai ye kahaani
rehtaa thaa kisi shehar mein ek aisa bhi insaan
jo naam ka muslim tha magar kaam ka shaitaan

zaalim ko zor e baazu pe apne gurur thaa
yaani ke bekhudi mein khuda se wo dur thaa
sab log use kehte thhe jallaad sitamgar
maasum ki fariyaad ka us pe na tha asar
jo waadaa us ne kar liyaa wo kar ke dikhaayaa
paison ke liye qatl kiye khun bahaya
ik din wo behtaa khun asar us pe kar gayaa
insaan zindaa ho gayaa shaitaan mar gayaa
allaah karam karna maula tu reham karna
allaah karam karna maula tu reham karna

imaan jise kehte hain farmaan e khuda hai
quraan ke har lafz mein us ki hi sadaa hai
allaah ne bakshi hai jo imaan ki daulat
ye sab se badi chiz hai insaan ki daulat
soye huye dilon ko jagata hai ye imaan
bhatke huyon ko raah dikhaataa hai ye imaan
imaan ki garmi se pighal jaate hain patthar
is nur se bante hain sanwarte hain muqaddar
jo sab se pyaar karta hai insaan wohi hai

muslim hai wohi saahib e imaan wohi hai
allaah karam karna maula tu reham karna
allaah karam karna maula tu reham karna

jis kaam ke karne pe na ho raazi koi dil
wo kaam bhi is duniya mein nafrat ke hai kaabil
jo kuchh bhi zubaan keh de wo iqraar nahin hai
laghzish hai labon ki wo gunehgaar nahin hai
jo dil se nahin karta buraai ka iraadaa
allaah se wo taubaa kare tod de waadaa
jaldi jo sambhal jaaye wo nadaan nahin hai
imaan jis mein ho wo beimaan nahin hai
duniya mein hameshaa to nahin rehtaa andheraa
insaan jahaan jaage wahin pe hai saveraa
allaah karam karna maula tu reham karna
allaah karam karna maula tu reham karna

jo sacche dil se karta hai imaan ki aarzu
allaah ki nazaron mein wo hotaa hai surkh ruh
imaan mein kya kya na sahaa pyaare nabi ne
kya aisi musibat bhi utthaayi hai kisi ne
karbal ke shahidon ne sabak hum ko padhaayaa
sajde mein de ke jaan ko imaan bachaayaa
iss raah mein jo sehte hain taqlif o musibat
ik roz un pe hoti hai allaah ki rehmat
insaan hai wo jo dusron ka dil na dukhaaye
pad jaaye agar jaan pe to jaan lutaaye
allaah karam karna maula tu reham karna
allaah karam karna maula tu reham karna.

ALLAH KARAM KARNA

dha	-	ti	ghe	dhin	-	dha	-	ti	ghe	dhin	-	dha	-	ti	ghe	dhin	-
1	2	3	4	5	6	1	2	3	4	5	6	1	2	3	4	5	6
																S'	-
																h	m
S'	-	S'	S'	-	S'	S'	-	S'	S'	S'	-	R'	-	S'	S'	N	-
s	b	ko	ne	-	k	ra	-	h	ch	la	-	na	-	me	re	a	l
N	-	D	-	D	-	D	-	D	D	D	-	P	-	P	P	P	D
la	-	-	-	bn	-	do	-	ko	bu	ra	-	ii	-	se	b	chha	-
N	-	D	P	M	-	M	P	G	-	G	-	G	-	G	M	P	-
na	-	me	re	a	l	la	-	-	-	a	l	la	-	h	k	r	m
M	-	M	P	G	-	G	-	G	M	P	-	M	-	M	-		
k	r	na	-	mau	-	la	-	tu	r	h	m	k	r	na	-		

interlude: 1 flute:

DNS'----- NS'R'S'R'---- N------

PNN---D---- PD--   D- M P-G M -

NDD- D- M P-G M -

dha	-	ti	ghe	dhin	-	dha	-	ti	ghe	dhin	-	dha	-	ti	ghe	dhin	-
																G	G
																i	k
G	-	G	G	-	G	G	-	G	R	S	-	S	M	M	M	M	-
va	-	k	ya	-	su	na	-	ti	hu	main	-	a	p	ni	zu	ba	-
M	P	G	-	G	G	G	-	G	G	-	G	G	-	G	R	S	-
ni	-	-	-	a	p	ne	-	b	do	-	se	main	-	ne	su	ni	-
M	-	M	M	M	-	M	-	-	-	D	D	D	-	D	D	D	-
hai	-	ye	k	ha	-	ni	-	-	-	r	h	ta	-	tha	ki	sii	-
D	D	D	D	D	D	N	-	D	D	D	-	D	-	-	-	P	-
sh	h	r	me	i	k	ae	-	sa	bhi	in	-	san	-	-	-	jo	-

P	-	P	P	P	P	P	-	P	M	M	M	S	M	M	M	M	-
na	-	m	ka	mu	k	li	m	tha	m	g	r	ka	-	m	ka	shai	-

M	-	-	-
tan	-	-	-

interlude: flute: S'<u>ND</u>P- <u>D</u>-M P-G M-

																S'	-
																za	-
S'	-	S'	S'	-	S'	S'	-	S'	S'	S'	S'	<u>N</u>	-	<u>D</u>	<u>N</u>	-	S'
li	m	ko	zo	-	re	ba	-	ju	pe	a	p	ne	-	gu	ru	-	r

S'	-	-	-	S'	-	S'	-	S'	S'	-	S'	S'	-	S'	S'	S'	-
tha	-	-	-	ya	-	ni	-	ki	be	-	khu	di	-	me	khu	da	-

<u>N</u>	-	<u>D</u>	<u>N</u>	-	S'	S'	-	-	-	P	P	<u>N</u>	-	<u>N</u>	<u>N</u>	<u>N</u>	-
se	-	vo	du	-	r	tha	-	-	-	s	b	lo	-	g	u	se	-

<u>N</u>	-	<u>N</u>	<u>N</u>	<u>D</u>	-	S'	-	<u>N</u>	<u>D</u>	<u>D</u>	-	<u>D</u>	-	-	-	P	-
k	h	te	the	j	l	la	-	d	si	t	m	gr	-	-	-	ma	-

P	-	P	P	P	P	P	-	P	P	M	S	M	-	M	M	-	M
su	-	m	ki	f	ri	ya	-	d	ka	u	s	pe	-	n	tha	-	a

M	-	-	-
sr	-	-	-

interlude: MM PP <u>DD</u> <u>NN</u> S'--

																S'	-
																jo	-
S'	-	S'	S'	-	S'	S'	-	S'	S'	S'	-	<u>N</u>	-	<u>D</u>	<u>N</u>	S'	-
va	-	da	u	s	ne	k	r	li	ya	vo	-	k	r	ke	di	kha	-

S'	-	-	-	S'	-	S'	-	S'	S'	S'	-	S'	-	S'	S'	S'	-
ya	-	-	-	pai	-	so	-	ke	li	ye	-	q	t	l	ki	ye	-

<u>N</u>	-	<u>D</u>	<u>N</u>	S'	-	S'	-	-	-	R'	R'	R'	R'	R'	R'	R'	R'
khu	-	n	b	ha	-	ya	-	-	-	i	k	di	n	vo	b	h	ta

S' R' R'	R' R' R'	R' R' S'	N - N	N D -	- P -
khu - n	a s r	u s pe	k r g	ya - -	- i n
P N N	N - N	D - D	P D -	N - D	P P M
sa - n	zin - da	ho - g	ya shai -	ta - n	m r g
M P G	- G -	G - G	M P -	M - M	P G -
ya - -	- a l	la - h	k r m	k r na	- mau -
G - G	M P -	M - M	-	interlude: 1	G -
la - tu	r h m	k r na	-		ii -
G - G	G G -	G - G	R S -	M - M	M M -
ma - n	ji se -	k h te	hain f r	ma - ne	khu da -
P - G	- G -	G - G	G G -	G - G	R S -
hai - -	- qu -	ra - n	ke h r	l f j	me u s
M - M	M M -	M - -	- D D	D - D	D D -
ki - hi	s da -	hai - -	- a l	la - h	ne b k
D - D	D D -	N - D	D D -	D - -	- P -
shi - hai	jo ii -	ma - n	ki dau -	l t -	- ye -
P - P	P P -	P - P	M M -	S - M	M M -
s b se	b di -	chi - z	hai in -	sa - n	ki dau -
M - -	- S' -	S' - S'	S' - S'	S' - S'	S' S' -
l t -	- so -	ye - hu	e - di	lo - ko	j ga -
N - D	N S' -	S' - -	- S' -	S' - S'	S' - S'
ta - hai	ye ii -	ma - n	- bh t	ke - hu	on - ko
S' - S'	S' S' -	N - D	N S' -	S' - -	- P -
ra - h	di kha -	ta - hai	ye ii -	ma - n	- ii -

Suman Kalyanpur 51 Songs' Sargam

Notes / Lyrics					
N - N	N N -	N - N	N N -	S' - N	D D -
ma - n	ki g r	mi - se	pi gh l	ja - te	hain p t
D - -	- P -	P - P	P P -	P - P	M S -
thr - -	- i s	nu - r	se b n	te - hain	sn v r
M - M	M M -	M - -	- S' -	S' S' S'	S' - S'
te - hain	mu q d	d r -	- jo -	s b se	pya - r
S' - S'	S' S' -	N - D	N S' -	S' - -	- P -
k r ta	hai i n	sa - n	v hi -	hai - -	- mu s
N - N	N N -	N - D	P P -	N - D	P P -
li m hai	vo hi -	sa - hi	be ii -	ma - n	v hi -
M P G	- G -	G - G	M P -	M - M	P G -
hai - -	- a l	la - h	k r m	k r na	- mau -
G - G	M P -	M - M	-		G G
la - tu	r h m	k r na			ji s
G - G	G G -	G - G	R S -	M - M	M M -
ka - m	ke k r	ne - se	n ra -	zi - ho	ko ii -
M P G	- G -	G - G	G G -	G - G	R S -
dil - -	- vo -	ka - m	bhi i s	du ni ya	me n f
M - M	M M -	M - -	- D -	D - D	D D -
r t ke	hai ka -	bil - -	- jo -	ku chh bhi	zu ba -
D - D	D D -	N - D	D D -	D - -	- P -
k h de	vo i q	ra - r	n hin -	hai - -	- l g
P - P	P P -	P - P	M M -	S M M	M M -
zi sh hai	l bo -	ki - vo	gu n h	ga - r	n hin -

M	-	-	-	S'	-	S'	-	S'	S'	S'	-	S'	-	S'	S'	S'	-
hai	-	-	-	jo	-	dil	-	se	n	hin	-	k	r	ta	bu	ra	-
N	-	D	N	S'	-	S'	-	-	-	S'	-	S'	-	S'	S'	S'	-
ii	-	ka	i	ra	-	da	-	-	-	a	l	la	-	h	se	vo	-
S'	-	S'	S'	S'	-	N	-	D	N	S'	-	S'	-	-	-	P	-
tau	-	ba	k	re	-	to	-	d	de	va	-	da	-	-	-	j	l
N	-	N	N	N	-	N	-	N	N	D	-	S'	-	N	D	D	-
di	-	jo	sn	bh	l	ja	-	ye	vo	na	-	da	-	n	n	hin	-
D	-	-	-	P	-	P	-	P	P	P	P	P	-	P	P		D
hai	-	-	-	ii	-	ma	-	n	ji	s	me	ho	-	vo	be	-	ii-
N	-	D	P	M	-	M	-	-	-	S'	-	S'	-	S'	S'	S'	-
ma	-	n	n	hin	-	hai	-	-	-	du	ni	ya	-	me	h	me	-
S'	-	S'	S'	S'	-	N	-	D	N	S'	-	S'	-	-	-	P	-
sha	-	to	n	hin	-	r	h	ta	an	dhe	-	ra	-	-	-	in	-
N	-	N	N	N	-	D	-	D	P	P	-	N	-	D	P	M	-
sa	-	n	j	ha	-	ja	-	ge	v	hin	-	pr	-	hai	s	ve	-
M	P	G	-	G	-	G	-	G	M	P	-	M	-	M	P	G	-
ra	-	-	-	a	l	la	-	h	k	rm	-	kr	-	na	-	mau	-
G	-	G	M	P	-	M	-	M	-								
la	-	tu	r	hm	-	kr	-	na	-								

further play like above.

6. AA HAM AHAD E VAFA KAR LEN

Film: Do Bhai (1969)
Lyrics: Anand Bakshi
Taal: Kaharwa

Music: Laxmikant Pyarelal
Singer: Md. Rafi, Suman K.
Chord: GPN   S=C

aa ham ahad e wafa kar lein, ye rasm ada kar lein
saamne aaj dono jahaan ke
aa ham ahad e wafa kar lein, ye rasm ada kar lein

veerano me bhi phool vo khil jaate hain, khilna hai jinhein -2
deewaren saari tod ke mil jaate hain milna hai jinhein
saamne, saamne is zamin aasmaan ke
aa ham ahad e wafa kar lein, ye rasm ada kar lein

dekho duayein deta hai hamko bhari bahaar ka dil -2
kahta hai ban ke phool khile tere mere pyar ka dil
saamne, saamne is hasiin gulsitaan ke
aa ham ahad e wafa kar lein, ye rasm ada kar lein
o....o.... o.... o.....
o....o.... o.... o.....
aa... aa... aa...

tumne banaa diya hai mohobbat mein bas deewaana mujhe
lagta hai ek jhuth zamane ka har fasaana mujhe
saamne, saamne aaj dono jahaan ke
aa ham ahad e wafa kar lein, ye rasm ada kar lein

AA HAM AHAD E VAFA KAR LEN

dha	ge	n	ti	n	ke	dhi	n	dha	ge	n	ti	n	ke	dhi	n
1	2	3	4	5	6	7	8	1	2	3	4	5	6	7	8
								N	-	-	-	N	S'	N	D
								aa	-	-	-	-	-	hm	-
P	P	N	P	G	D	D	P	P	-	-	-	-	-	P	-
a	h	de	v	fa	-	k	r	le	-	-	-	-	-	ye	-
R	G	P	G	R	G	P	D	N	-	-	-	N	S'	N	D
r	s	m	a	da	-	k	r	le	-	-	-	aa	-	h	m
P	P	N	P	G	-	D	P	P	-	G	-	-	-	P	-
a	h	de	v	fa	-	k	r	le	-	-	-	-	-	ye	-
R	G	P	G	R	G	P	D	N	-	-	-	-	-	N	R'
r	s	m	a	da	-	k	r	le	-	-	-	-	-	sa	m
R'	S'	-	-	-	-	N	R'	R'	S'	N	R'	R'	S'	D	S'
ne	-	-	-	-	-	aa	j	do	-	no	j	ha	-	ke	-
N	-	-	-	N	S'	N	D	P	P	N	P	G	D	D	P
aa	-	-	-	-	-	hm	-	a	h	de	v	fa	-	k	r
P	-	G	-	-	-	P	R	R	G	P	G	R	G	P	D
le	-	-	-	-	-	ye	-	r	s	m	a	da	-	k	r
N	-	-	-												
le	-	-	-												

interlude: R' R' R' R' R'R'R' R' S' N

S'	-	S'	-	S'	S'	-	S'	N	R'	S'	R'	N	N	N	N
vi	-	ra	-	no	me	-	bhi	fu	-	-	-	l	vo	khi	l
D	S'	N	-	D	D	D	D	P	N	D	-	P	P	P	-
ja	-	-	-	te	hain	khi	l	na	-	-	-	hai	ji	nhe	-

S'	-	S'		S'	S'	-	S'	S'	G'	R'	-	S'	S'	N	N
di	-	va	-	ren	sa	-	ri	to	-	-	-	d	ke	mi	l
D	S'	N	-	D	D	D	D	P	N	D	-	P	P	P	-
ja	-	-	-	te	hain	mi	l	na	-	-	-	hain	ji	nhe	-
-	-	-	-	-	-	N	-S'	R'	M'	G'	-	G'	-	R'	-
-	-	-	-	-	-	sa	-m	ne	-	-	-	-	-	-	-
-	-	-	-	-	-	N	R'	R'	S'	-	-	-	-	N	R'
-	-	-	-	-	-	sa	-m	ne	-	-	-	-	-	is	j
R'	S'	N	-R'	S'	-	D	S'	N	-	-	-	N	S'	N	D
mi	-	aa	-s	ma	-	ke	-	aa	-	-	-	-	-	hm	-
P	P	N	P	G	D	D	P	P	-	G	-	-	-	P	-
a	h	de	v	fa	-	k	r	le	-	-	-	-	-	ye	-
R	G	P	G	R	G	P	D	N	-	-	-	N	S'	N	D
r	s	m	a	da	-	k	r	le	-	-	-	aa	-	h	m
P	P	N	P	G	D	D	P	P	-	G	-	-	-	P	-
a	h	de	v	fa	-	k	r	le	-	-	-	-	-	ye	-
R	G	P	G	R	G	P	D	N	-	-	-	-	-		
r	s	m	a	da	-	k	r	le	-	-	-	-	-		

N- N- N- NS' NS' DN—N- NS'D—

o------------------------------

NS'NS'DN—N—S'ND-   DNDNGP-

o---------------------   aa-------

S'	-	S'	-	S'	S'	-	S'	N	R'	S'	-	N	N	N	-
tum	-	ne	-	b	na	-	di	ya	-	-	-	hai	mo	ho	-

D	S'	N	-	D	D	D	D	P	N	D	-	P	P	P	-
bt	-	-	-	me	b	s	di	va	-	-	-	na	mu	jhe	-
S'	S'	S'		S'	S'	-	S'	N	R'	S'	-	N	N	N	-
l	g	ta	-	hai	e	-	k	jhu	-	-	-	th	z	ma	-
D	S'	N	-	D	D	D	D	P	N	D	-	P	P	P	-
ne	-	-	-	ka	h	r	f	sa	-	-	-	na	mu	jhe	-
-	-	-	-	-	-	N	-S'	R'	M'	G'	M'	R'	-	-	-
-	-	-	-	-	-	sa	-m	ne	-	-	-	-	-	-	-
-	-	-	-	-	-	N	R'	R'	S'	-	-	-	-	N	R'
-	-	-	-	-	-	sa	-m	ne	-	-	-	-	-	aa	j
R'	S'	N	R'	R'	S'	D	S'	N	-	-	-	N	S'	N	D
do	-	no	j	ha	-	ke	-	aa	-	-	-	-	-	hm	-
P	P	N	P	G	D	D	P	P	-	G	-	-	-	P	-
a	h	de	v	fa	-	k	r	le	-	-	-	-	-	ye	-
R	G	P	G	R	G	P	D	N	-	-	-				
r	s	m	a	da	-	k	r	le	-	-	-				

7.   AAJKAL TERE MERE PYAR KE CHARCHE

Film: Brahmchari (1968)
Lyrics: Shailendra
Taal: Kaharwa

Music: Shanker Jaikishan
Singer: Md. Rafi, Suman K.
Chord: P$\underline{N}$R'   S=C

aajkal tere mere pyar ke charche har zubaan par
sab ko maloom hai aur sabko khabar ho gayi

(humne to pyar mein aisa kaam kar liya
pyar ki raah mein apna naam kar liya) -2
pyar ki raah mein apna naam kar liya
aajkal tere mere pyar.......

(do badan ek dil ek jaan ho gaye
manzilen ek hui humsafar ban gaye) -2
manzilen ek hui humsafar ban gaye
aajkal tere mere pyar...

(kyon bhala hum daren dil ke malik hain hum
har janam mein tujhe apna mana sana)-2
har janam mein tujhe apna mana sanam
aajkal tere mere pyar...

AAJKAL TERE MERE PYAR KE CHARCHE

dhin tete dhindhin	dhin tete dhindhin	dhintete dhin dhin	dhin tetedhindhin
1 2 3 4	5 6 7 8	1 2 3 4	5 6 7 8

prelude:

guitar: NS'ND   NS'ND N –

NS'ND NS'R'G' G'R'S'N S'R'G'M'

M'G'R'S' M'M' G'G' R'R' S'-

S'G'R'S'NDPM

M –N M –MN-   M –N M –MN-   M –N M –MN- N---

synthe: N S' R'----   R'G'P'M'G'M'- P'M'P'M'G'—G'M'G'R'---

S'R'S'N-- P—D NS'NDN

accordian: S'DNR'--- G'M'P'M'G'M'---

M'M'P'M'G'--- G'M'G'R'—S'R'S'N

P –D NS'NDN--

guitar: M –N M –MN-   M –N M –MN-   M –N M –MN- N---

			-N -N S'
			-aa -j kl

R' R' R' R',R'	R' R' S' N	P -P P (N	R') - D N
teremerepya r,ke	ch rche hr z	ba -n pr (a	chha) - sb ko

S' S' S' S'	S' R' -P D	N -N N (R'	N)
ma lum hai aur	sb ko -kh br	ho -g yi (to	kya)

interlude: saxophone:

M'M'M'M' G' –G'M'-- G'M' G'M'

R'R'R'R' S' –S'R' -- S'R' S'R'

NNNN D –DN DN DN

NNNN D –DN DN DN

synthe:

N S'R' N G' R'G' R' N

NNNN NNNN N

												-M	-P
												-hm	-ne
M	-	-M	-P	M	-	-M	-P	N	-	-D	-S'	N	-	-S'	-R'
to	-	-pya	-r	me	-	-ae	-sa	ka	-	m,kr	-li	ya	-	-pya	-r
S'	-	-S'	-R'	S'	-	-R'	G'	M'	-	-D	-S'	N	-	-G'	-M'
ki	-	-ra	-h	me	-	-a	pna	na	-	m,kr	-li	ya	-	-pya	-r
G'	-	-R'	-G'	R'	-	-S'	N	R'	-	-S'	-N	N	-		
ki	-	-ra	-h	me	-	-a	pna	na	-	m,kr	-li	ya	-		

8.   AAP SE HAMKO BICHHDE HUE

Film: Vishwas (1969)   Music: Kalyanji Anandji
Lyrics: Gulshan Bawra   Singer: Manhar Udas, Suman K.
Taal: Kaharwa dugun   Chord: MDS'   S=D

apase hamako bichhade huye, ek jamaana bit gaya
apana mukaddar bigade huye, ek jamaana bit gaya

apase milake in ankhon ne kitane khwaab sajaaye the
jis gulashan men hamane milake git wafa ke gaaye the
us gulashan ko ujade huye, ek jamaana bit gaya

kismat hamako le ayi hai gulashan se wiraane men
ansu bhi naakaam rahe hain dil ki ag bujhaane men
is wiraane men jalate huye, ek jamaana bit gaya

AAP SE HAMKO BICHHDE HUE

dhage	nti	nke dhin	dhage	nti	nke dhin	dhage	nti	nke dhin	dhage	nti	nke dhin
12	34	56 78	12	34	56 78	12	34	56 78	12	34	56 78

prelude:

M′ G′ G̲′ R′ R̲′ S′ -2

S R̲ G G D̲ –

D̲ D̲ P P M M M   D̲ D̲ P P M - -

M S G M P N̲ - S′ N̲ D̲ M P –

D̲ D̲ P P M M M   D̲ D̲ P P M - -

	M	-M -M	M	P	M G	M	MD̲	- P	D̲	-	(P M)
	aa	-p -se	hm	-	ko -	bi	chhde	- hu	e	-	- -
-	D̲	-N̲ -N	N	N̲	D̲ P	D̲	P	M G	M	-	- -
-	e	-k -z	ma	-	na -	bi	-	t g	ya	-	- -
-	M	-M -M	M	P	M G	M	MD̲	- P	D̲	-	(P M)
-	ap	na mu	q	-	dd r	bi	gde	- hu	e	-	- -
-	D̲	-N̲ -N	N	N̲	D̲ P	D̲	P	M G	M	-	- -
-	e	-k -z	ma	-	na -	bi	-	t g	ya	-	- -

interlude: M N ------ N̲ D̲ N N̲ ---

D̲ N – N̲ – D̲ N ᴰN - D̲ PD̲ M -

	S′	-R̲′ -S′	N̲	N̲	N̲ -	N	NN̲	-D̲ P	M	- M	-
	aa	-p -se	mi	l	ke -	-	in	-aan -	khon	- ne	-
-	S′S′	-R̲′ S′	N̲	-	N̲ N̲	NN̲	N̲	D̲ P	M	- -	-
-	kit	-ne -	kha	-	b s	ja-	-	ye -	the	- -	-
-	S′S′	-R̲′ -S′	N̲	N̲	N̲ -	N	NN̲	-D̲ P	M	M M	-
-	jis	-gu -l	sh	n	me -	-	hm	-ne -	mi	l ke	-
-	S′	-R̲′ -S′	N̲	-	N̲ -	N	NN̲	-D̲ P	M	- -	-
-	gi	-t -v	fa	-	ke -	-	ga-	-ye -	the	- -	-

S	M	M	M	M	P	M	G	MM	-D	-	P	D	-	P	M
u	s	gu	l	sh	n	ko	-	uj	-de	-	hu	e	-	-	-
-	M	-M	-M	MP	-	M	G	MM	-D	-	P	D	-	-	-
-	us	-gu	-l	shn	-	ko	-	uj	-de	-	hu	e	-	-	-
-	D	-N	-N	N	N	D	P	D	P	M	G	M	-	-	-
-	e-	-k	-z	ma	-	na	-	bi	-	t	g	ya	-	-	-

interlude: M N ------ N D N N ---

D N – N – D N ᴰN - D PD M –

S'S'R'S' N NN NN DPM M
kismt   hm ko- le- aa-yi hai

S'-R'S' N   N NNNDP   M
gulshn se vira------ne- me

S'R'S'   N   N NND PM M
aansu- bhi naka--m rhe hain

S'S' R'S' NN NNNNDP   M
dil ki-   aag bujha-----ne- me

MM M MPPM G   MD PD (PM)
Is   vira—ne- me jlte huye -2

DN NNNDP DPM GM
ek zma-na- bi-t   gya

9. AAYA NA HAMKO PYAR JATANA

Film: Pahchaan (1970)   Music: Shanker Jaikishan
Lyrics: Indeevar   Singer: Mukesh, Suman K.
Taal: Kaharwa   Chord: GPN MDS' S=C#

M: aya na hamako pyaar jataana pyaar kabhi se tujhe karate hain
S: bholaapan tera bha gaya hamako saadagi par teri marate hain

M: jisane hamaare dil ko samajha wo ek tera hi dil hai
    tera anchal, teri baahen, <u>apani yahin to mnjil hai -2</u>
    ham to tere ho hi chuke hain apana kahate darate hain
S: bholaapan tera bha gaya hamako saadagi par teri marate hain

S: surat achchhi, sirat achchhi tu to ek hai laakhon men
    dil karata hai dil se laga lun rakh lun chhupa ke ankhon men
    khud pe bharosa badh jaata hai jab tere saath gujrate hain

M: ek hi jiwan men to dil ki pyaas bujha nahin paayenge
S: tujhako fir paane ke liye ham fir duniya men ayenge
B: pyaar amar hai amar hi rahega, marane do insaan marate hain

S: bholaapan tera bha gaya hamako saadagi par teri marate hain
M: aya na hamako pyaar jataana pyaar kabhi se tujhe karate hain
S: bholaapan tera bha gaya hamako saadagi par teri marate hain

AAYA NA HAMKO PYAR JATANA

dha	ge	n	ti	n	ke	dhi	n	dha	ge	n	ti	n	ke	dhi	n
1	2	3	4	5	6	7	8	1	2	3	4	5	6	7	8

prelude:

S' N D - PD ND S'N R'S'- PS' DPMD

PS'--- S'NR'- S'N

S' G' R' S' N D P M   M P D N S'-

N	D	D	D	D	-	P	N	N	-	-	D	D	-	D	-
aa	-	ya	n	h	m	ko	-	pya	-	r	j	ta	-	na	-

S'	-	-	N	D	P	M	D	P	-	M	-	G	-	-	-
pya	-	-r	k	bhi	se	tu	jhe	k	r	te	-	hain	-	-	-

P	-	P	M*	P	-	P	N	N	-	D	D	D	-	D	-
bho	-	la	-	pn	-	te	ra	bha	-	g	ya	h	m	ko	-

S'	G'	G'	G'	R'	R'	S'	N	S'	-	N	-	D	-	^{M}P	G
sa	-	d	gi	p	r	te	re	m	r	te	-	hain	-	-	-

interlude:

D N P D N S' R' G'   G' P' M' R' G'-

G' G' G' M'- R'G'   S' S' S' R'- NS'

D' D' D' D'—P' D' P' M' G' M'—G' M' G' R' S'- DS' R' G'-

S'	N	N	N	N	-	N	-	S'	N	N	-	S'	N	N	-
ji	s	ne	h	ma	-	re	-	di	l	ko	-	s	m	jha	-

P	N	N	N	N	-	N	S'	R'	S'	N	D	D	-	-	-
vo	-	e	k	te	-	ra	-	hi	-	di	l	hai	-	-	-

D	S'	S'	-	S'	-	S'	N	R'	-	S'	-	S'	-	S'	-
te	-	ra	-	aan	-	ch	l	te	-	ri	-	ba	-	he	-

S'	G'	G'	R'	S'	-	D	N	S'	-	N	D	P	-	-	-
a	p	ni	y	hi	-	to	-	mn	-	zi	l	hai	-	-	-

P	S'	S'	N	D	-	M	D	P	-	M	G	G	-	-	-
a	p	ni	y	hi	-	to	-	mn	-	zi	l	hai	-	-	-

N	D	D	-	D	-	P	N	N	-	D	D	D	-	D	-
h	m	to	-	te	-	re	-	ho	-	hi	chu	ke	-	hain	-

P	S'	S'	-	D	P	M	D	P	-	M	-	G	-	-	-
a	p	na	-	k	h	te	-	d	r	te	-	hain	-	-	-

P	-	P	M*	P	-	P	N	N	-	D	D	D	-	D	-
bho	-	la	-	pn	-	te	ra	bha	-	g	ya	h	m	ko	-

S'	G'	G'	G'	R'	R'	S'	N	S'	-	N	-	D	-	ᴹP	G
sa	-	d	gi	p	r	te	re	m	r	te	-	hain	-	-	-

interlude:

DPNP x 3 G-   NDNP x 3 G-

GM MP PD- DNS'R'G'- GM MP PD-

R'---- NS' DNPN

S'------ DN—PD---

S'	N	N	N	N	-	N	-	P	N	N	N	S'	R'	R'	-
su	-	r	t	a	ch	chhi	-	sii	-	r	t	a	ch	chhi	-

N	R'	R'		S'	-	S'	S'	N	D	N	P	D	-	-	-
tu	-	to	-	e	-	k	hai	la	-	khon	-	me	-	-	-

G	G	G	-	R	-	S	R	G	<u>D</u>	<u>D</u>	<u>D</u>	<u>D</u>	D	D	-
di	l	k	r	ta	-	hai	-	di	l	se	l	ga	-	lu	-

D	S'	S'	S'	G'	-	G'	-	R'	-	S'	N	D	-	-	-
r	kh	lu	chhu	pa	-	ke	-	aan	-	khon	-	me	-	-	-

N	D	D	D	D	-	D	P	N	D	D	-	D	-	D	-
khu	d	pe	bh	ro	-	sa	-	b	dh	ja	-	ta	-	hai	-

D	S'	S'	N	D	P	M	D	P	-	M	-	G	-	-	-
j	b	te	re	sa	-	th	gu	z	r	te	-	hain	-	-	-

```
P   -   P   M* | P   -   P   N  | N   -   D   D  | D   -   D   -
bho -   la  -  | pn  -   te  ra | bha -   g   ya | h   m   ko  -

S'  G'  G'  G' | R'  R'  S'  N  | S'  -   N   -  | D   -   ᴹP  G
sa  -   d   gi | p   r   te  re | m   r   te  -  | hain -   -   -
```

interlude:

```
D N P D N S' R' G'     G' P' M' R' G'-
G' G' G' M'- R'G'     S' S' S' R'- NS'
D' D' D' D'—P' D' P' M' G' M'—G' M' G' R' S'- DS' R' G'-
```

```
S'  N   N   N  | N   -   N   N  | S'  N   N   -  | S'  N   N   -
e   -   k   hi | ji  -   v   n  | me  -   to  -  | di  l   ki  -

P   N   N   N  | N   -   N   S' | R'  S'  N   D  | D   -   -   -
pya -   s   bu | jha -   n   hin| pa  -   yen -  | ge  -   -   -

G   G   G   -  | R   S   S   R  | G   D̲   D̲   D̲  | D̲   D   D   -
tu  jh  ko  -  | fi  r   pa  -  | ne  -   ke  li | e   -   hm  -

D   S'  S'  S' | G'  -   G'  -  | R'  -   S'  N  | D   -   -   -
fi  r   du  ni | ya  -   me  -  | aa  -   yen -  | ge  -   -   -

N   D   D   D  | D   D   D   P  | N   D   D   D  | D   -   D   -
pya -   r   a  | m   r   hai a  | m   r   hi  r  | he  -   ga  -

P   S'  S'  N  | D   -   M   D  | P   -   M   -  | G   -   -   -
m   r   ne  ko | in  -   san -  | m   r   te  -  | hain -   -   -

P   -   P   M* | P       P   N  | N   -   D   D  | D   -   D   -
bho -   la  -  | pn  -   te  ra | bha -   g   ya | h   m   ko  -

S'  G'  G'  G' | R'  R'  S'  N  | S'  -   N   -  | D   -   ᴹP  G
sa  -   d   gi | p   r   te  re | m   r   te  -  | hain -   -   -

N   -   D   D  | D   -   P   N  | N   -   -   D  | D   -   D   -
aa  -   ya  n  | h   m   ko  -  | pya -   r   j  | ta  -   na  -
```

S'	-	-	N	D	P	M	D	P	-	M	-	G	-	-	-
pya	-	-r	k	bhi	se	tu	jhe	k	r	te	-	hain	-	-	-

P	-	P	M*	P	-	P	N	N	-	D	D	D	-	D	-
bho	-	la	-	pn	-	te	ra	bha	-	g	ya	h	m	ko	-

S'	G'	G'	G'	R'	R'	S'	N	S'	-	N	-	D	-	ᴹP	G
sa	-	d	gi	p	r	te	re	m	r	te	-	hain	-	-	-

10. BAHNA NE BHAI KI KALAI SE

Film: Resham ki Dor (1974) Music: Shanker Jaikishan
Lyrics: Shailendra Singer: Suman K.
Taal: Kaharwa Chord: RMD MDS' S=C#

bahana ne bhaai ki kalaai se pyaar baandha hai
pyaar ke do taar se snsaar baandha hai
resham ki dori se-3 snsaar baandha hai

sundarata men jo kanhaiya hai mamata men yashoda maiyya hai
wo aur nahin duja koi wo te mera raaja bhaiyya hai
bahana ne bhaai ki kalaai se pyaar baandha hai

mera ful hai tu, talawaar hai tu meri laaj ka paharedaar hai tu
main akeli kahaan is duniya men mera saara snsaar hai tu
bahana ne bhaai ki kalaai se pyaar baandha hai

hamen dur bhale kismat kar de apane man se n juda karana
saawan ke paawan din bhaiyya bahana ko yaad kiya karana
bahana ne bhaai ki kalaai se pyaar baandha hai

BAHNA NE BHAI KI KALAI SE

dha	ge	n	ti	n	ke	dhi	n	dha	ge	n	ti	n	ke	dhi	n
1	2	3	4	5	6	7	8	1	2	3	4	5	6	7	8
prelude: G P D N N --- P N N—NDPMGR--															
	D	D	D	D	D	D	N	D	D	D	-	R	M	P	D
	bh	na	ne	bha	ii	ki	k	la	ii	se	-	-	-	-	-
-	D	D	D	D	D	D	N	D	D	D	-	P	-M	MP	D
-	bh	na	ne	bha	ii	ki	k	la	ii	se	-	pya	-r	ba-	dha
P	-	-	-	-	N	N	D	P	M	G	G	P	-M	G	G
hai	-	-	-	-	pya	r,ke	do	ta	-r	se	sn	sa	-r	ba	dha
R	-	-	-	-	S'	S'	S'	N	N	D	P	-	N	N	D
hai	-	-	-	-	re	shm	ki	do	ri	se	-	-	re	shm	ki
M	D	P	M	-	N	N	D	P	M	G	G	P	-M	G	G
do	ri	se	-	-	re	shm	ki	do	ri	se	sn	sa	-r	ba	dha
R	-	-	-	-											
hai	-	-	-	-											

interlude: 1

M' G' R'--- S'R'G'M'G' S'--   R'S' S'N ND   DNG'R'S'NPMR—
RR MM GG M—DD MM GG R
RR MM GG M—DD MM G- R-

														S'	N
														sun	-
S'	S'	S'	N	S'	-	S'	S'	R'	S'	N	D	D	-	N	D
d	r	ta	-	me	-	jo	k	nhai	-	ya	-	hai	-	m	m
N	-	N	D	N	-	N	-	M	-	N	D	D	-	S'	-
ta	-	me	y	sho	-	da	-	main	-	ya	-	hai	-	vo	-

S'	-	S'	S'	N	-	P	D	S'	-	N	-	N	-	N	N
au	-	r	n	hin	-	du	-	ja	-	ko	-	ii	-	vo	to

N	-	N	-	M	-	D	-	-	M	-G	R	R	-	-	-
me	-	ra	-	ra	-	ja	-	-	bhai	-ya	-	hai	-	-	-

interlude: 2

PD<u>N</u>S'R'—R'<u>G</u>'R'--- R'<u>G</u>'R'S'- S'R'S'<u>N</u>- <u>N</u>S'<u>N</u>D- PDPM- P- D-
MPM<u>G</u> M- P- <u>G</u>MP P-M- <u>G</u>R
R'<u>G</u>'M'P'D'—M'D'P'<u>G</u>'R'—M'- <u>G</u>'R'S'---

														S'	N
														me	ra

S'	-	S'	N	S'	-	S'	S'	R'	S'	N	D	D	-	N	D
fu	-	l	hai	tu	-	t	l	va	-	r	hai	tu	-	me	ri

N	-	N	D	N	N	N	-	M	-	N	D	D	-	S'	N
la	-	j	ka	p	h	re	-	da	-	r	hai	tu	-	main	a

S'	-	S'	R'	N	-	P	D	S'	S'	N	-	N	-	N	-
ke	-	li	k	ha	-	i	s	du	ni	ya	-	me	-	me	-

N	-	N	-	M	-	D	-	-	M	-G	-R	R	-	-	-
ra	-	sa	-	ra	-	sn	-	-	sa	-r	-hai	tu	-	-	-

interlude: 1 play

S'N	S'S'	NS'	S'S'R'S'	<u>NN</u>	D
hme	dur	bhle	kismt	kr	de

<u>N</u>D<u>N</u>	<u>N</u>D	N	N	PRM	<u>N</u>DD
apne	mn	se	n	juda	krna

S'NS'	S'	<u>N</u>-PD	S'	<u>NN</u>
savn	ke	pa-vn	din	bhaiya

<u>NN</u>	N	MD	D	M	<u>G</u>-R
bhna	ko	yad	kiya	krna	

11. BAAD MUDDAT KE YE GHADI AAYI

Film: Jahan Aara (1964)
Lyrics: Rajendra Krishna
Taal: Kaharwa

Music: Madan Mohan
Singer: Md. Rafi, Suman K.
Chord: SGP   S=D#

Rafi: baad muddat ke yah ghadi aayi ap aye to jindagi aayi
ishq mar-mar ke kaamayaab hua aaj ek zrra afataab hua

Suman: shukriya ai hujur ane ka wakt jaaga garibakhaane ka
ek jmaane ke baad did hui id se pahale meri id hui

Rafi: id ka chaand aj dekha hai id ka kyon na aitabaar aaye
hath uthakar dua yah karta hun id fir aisi bar-bar aaye
din jmaane ka, raat apani hai is ghadi kaayanaat apani hai
ishq par husn ki inayat hai mere pahalu men meri jnnat hai

Suman: faasale waqt ne mita hi die dil tadpate huye mila hi diye
kaash is waqt maut aa jaaye zindagani pe aake chha jaaye

Both: baad muddat ke yah ghadi aayi ap aye to jindagi aayi
ishq mar-mar ke kaamayaab hua aj ek jrra afataab hua

BAAD MUDDAT KE YE GHADI AAYI

dha	ge	n	ti	n	ke	dhi	n	dha	ge	n	ti	n	ke	dhi	n
1	2	3	4	5	6	7	8	1	2	3	4	5	6	7	8
prelude: G M D M G G M D M R G M P G S															
G M R R P --- N D S'--- P G P M G M G R --															
								G				R	G	M	P
								ba				-	d	mu	-
M	-	G	-	R	.N	-	S	G	R	G	-	GM	P	M	-
d	-	-	t	ke	ye	-	gh	di	-	-	-	aa-	-	yi	-
G	R	-	G	R	G	M	P	M	G	-	-	R	.N	-	S
-	-	-	aa	-	p	aa	-	ye	-	-	-	to	zin	-	d
R	G	-	R	M	P	M	-	G	-	-	P	-	P	D	N
gi	-	-	-	aa	-	yi	-	-	-	-	i	sh	q	m	r
S'	-	-	-	S'	N	-	P	M	R	G	-	M	P	M	-
mr	-	-	-	ke	ka	-	m	ya	-	-	-	b	hu	aa	-
G	R	-	G	R	G	M	P	M	-	G	-	R	.N	-	S
-	-	-	aa	-	j	i	k	z	-	r	-	ra	aa	-	f
G	R	G	-	M	P	M	-	G	-	-	G	R	G	N	D
ta	-	-	-	b	hu	aa	-	-	-	-	aa	-	j	i	k
M	-	G	-	R	.N	-	S	G	R	G	-	M	P	M	-
z	-	r	-	ra	aa	-	f	ta	-	-	-	b	hu	aa	-
G	-	-	G	R	G	M	P	M	-	G	-	R	.N	-	S
-	-	-	shu	k	ri	ya	-	hai	-	-	-	hu	zu	-	r
G	R	G	-	M	P	M	-	G	R	-	P	P	P	D	N
aa	-	-	-	ne	-	ka	-	-	-	-	shu	k	ri	ya	-

Suman Kalyanpur 51 Songs' Sargam

S'	-	-	-	S'	N̲	-	P	MG	R	-	G	M	P	M	-
hai	-	-	-	hu	zu	-	r	aa-	-	-	-	ne	-	ka	-
G	R	-	G	R	G	M	P	M	-	G	-	R	.N	-	S
-	-	-	v	-	qt	ja	-	ga	-	-	-	g	ri	-	b
G	R	G	-	M	P	M	-	G	-	-	D	D	D	D	-
kha	-	-	-	ne	-	ka	-	-	-	-	i	k	z	ma	-
S'	N̲	S'	-	D	D	G	P	S'	-	P	-	G	P	M	-
ne	-	-	-	ke	ba	-	d	ii	-	-	-	d	hu	ii	-
G	-	-	G	R	G	M	P	M	M	G	-	R	.N	-	S
-	-	-	ii	-	d	se	-	p	h	-	-	le	me	-	ri
G	R	G	-	M	P	M	-	G	-	-	G	R	G	M	N̲
ii	-	-	-	d	hu	ii	-	-	-	-	ii	-	d	se	-
M	M	G	-	R	.N	-	S	G	R	G	-	M	P	M	-
p	h	-	-	le	me	-	ri	ii	-	-	-	d	hu	ii	-
G	-	-	G	-	P	D	N̲	D	-	-	-	D	P	-	M
-	-	-	ii	-	d	ka	-	chan	-	-	-	d	aa	-	j
MG	R	-	-	P	-	P	-	-	-	-	P	G	P	S'	-
de-	-	-	-	kha	-	hai	-	-	-	-	ii	-	d	ka	-
N̲	-	N̲	P	-	P	G	P	P	N̲-	-	D	N	-	S'	-
kyu	-	na	-	-	ae	-	t	ba	-	-	r	aa	-	ye	-
-	-	-	N	-	N	N	-	S'	S'	-	-	S'	N̲	-	P
-	-	-	ha	-th	u	tha	-	k	r	-	-	du	aa	-	ye
MG	R	G	-	M	P	M	-	G	-	-	G	R	G	M	P
k-	r	-	-	ta	-	hu	-	-	-	-	ii	-	d	fi	r

M	-	G	-	R	.N	-	S	G	R	G	-	GM	P	M	-
ae	-	sii	-	-	ba	-	r	ba	-	-	r	aa-	-	ye	-

G	-	-	G	R	G	<u>N</u>	D	M	-	G	-	R	.N	-	S
-	-	-	ii	-	d	fi	r	ae	-	sii	-	-	ba	-	r

G	R	G	-	GM	P	M	-	G	-
ba	-	-	r	aa-	-	ye	-	-	-

```
 G      PNS'<u>ND</u>     P   MM  GGR GMP   P
din  zma—ne- ka  rat  ap- ni--    hai

GG    PDNS'      <u>N</u>DPSR    PPM*  P
is    ghdi--- qa-ynat   apni  hai

DD    DD <u>N</u>DS'D   G   PDNS'-P GP  M  G
ishq  pr  hu---sn  ki   ina------ yt  hai—

 GRG   MPM  G   R.NS   GRGMP  M  G
me-re phlu  me  me--ri  j--nnt   hai—

GRG      <u>N</u>DM  G   R.NS   GRGMP  M  G
me-re phlu  me  me--ri  j--nnt    hai—

G PNS'   PP   R   GP    M*  M*P
fasle-  v-qt  ne  mita  hi   diye

G   PNS'P  PS   RP    M*  M*P
dil  tdpte  hue  mila  hi   diye

DD    DD  <u>N</u>DS'  DGP    S'  GPM  G
kash is   v--qt  mau-t  aa  ja-e—

GRG MPMG  R   .NS   GRG      MPM  G -
zin-dgani-  pe  aake  chha-- ja-e—
GRG<u>N</u>DMG  R   .NS   GRG      MPM  G -
zindga--ni  pe   aake  chha-- ja-e--
```

12. BUJHA DIYE HAIN KHUD APNE HATHO

Film: Shagun (1964)
Lyrics: Sahir Ludhiyanvi
Taal: Kaharwa

Music: khaiyyam
Singer: Suman K.
Chord: GPN MDS' S=C#

bujha diye hain khud apane haathon mohabbaton ke diye jala ke
meri wafa ne ujaad di hai ummid ki bastiyaan basa ke

tujhe bhula denge apane dil se ye faisala to kiya hai lekin
na dil ko maalum hai na hamako jienge kaise tujhe bhula ke

kabhi milenge jo raaste men to munh firaakar palat padenge
kahin sunenge jo naam tera to chup rahenge najr jhuka ke

na sochane par bhi sochati hun ke zindagaani men kya rahega
teri tamanna ko dafn kar ke tere khyaalon se dur jaake

BUJHA DIYE HAIN KHUD APNE HATHO

dha	-	tin	tin	ta	-	dhin	dhin	dha	-	tin	tin	ta	-	dhin	dhin
1	2	3	4	5	6	7	8	1	2	3	4	5	6	7	8

prelude: M'----- G'S'G'-----

| G | D | - | M | P | - | G | - | M | M | D | D | PD | <u>N</u> | P | - |
| bu | jha | - | di | ye | - | hain | - | khud | a | p | ne | ha- | - | tho | - |

| - | N | N | N | D | N | P | - | M* | M* | - | G | M* | P | P | - |
| - | mo | h | bb | to | - | ke | - | di | ye | - | j | la | - | ke | - |

flute: G- MDP- G S G--

| G | D | - | M | P | - | G | - | M | D | - | P | PD | <u>N</u> | P | - |
| me | ri- | - | v | fa | - | ne | - | u | ja | - | d | di- | - | hai | - |

| N | N | - | N | D | N | P | - | M* | M* | - | G | M* | P | P | - |
| um | mi | - | d | ki | - | b | s | ti | ya | - | b | sa | - | ke | - |

interlude: G--- M PDS'----S'---N---

  D N S' N P---   G--- P M*DP--

| P | DN | S' | S' | S' | - | N | - | D | D | D | <u>D</u> | DN | S' | S' | |
| tu | jhe- | - | bhu | la | - | de | - | ge | a | p | ne | dil- | - | se | - |

| R' | R' | - | S' | N | - | R' | - | N | D | - | P | P | - | P | |
| ye | fai | - | s | la | - | to | - | ki | ya | - | hai | le | - | kin | - |

music: G – MPN—DPMGP--

| G | D | - | M | P | - | G | - | M | D | - | D | PD | <u>N</u> | P | - |
| n | dil | - | ko | ma | - | lu | - | m | hai | - | n | hm | - | ko | - |

| N | N | - | N | D | N | P | - | M* | M* | - | G | M* | P | P | - |
| ji | yen | - | ge | kai | - | se | - | tu | jhe | - | bhu | la | - | ke | - |

interlude: G--- M PDS'----S'---N---

    D N S' N P---   G--- P M*DP--

| P | DN | S' | S' | S' | - | N | - | D | D | - | D | DN | S' | S' | |
| k | bhi- | - | mi | le | - | ge | - | jo | ra | - | s | te- | - | me | - |

| R' | R' | - | S' | N | - | R' | - | N | D | - | P | P | - | P | |
| to | muh | - | fi | ra | - | kr | - | p | l | t | p | den | - | ge | - |

G	D	-	M	P	-	G	-	M	D	-	P	PD	N	P	-
k	hin	-	su	ne	-	ge	-	jo	na	-	m	te-	-	ra	-
-	N	N	N	D	N	P	-	M*	M*	-	G	M*	P	P	-
-	to	chup	r	hen	-	ge	-	n	zr	-	jhu	ka	-	ke	-

interlude: P—M* PDS--- M* PDG—D---

D	D	-	D	D	-	D	-	D	D	-	D	DN	S'	D	
n	so	-	ch	ne	-	pr	-	bhi	so	-	ch	ti-	-	hu	-
D	D	-	P	N	-	D	-	P	DP	N	D	M*	D	P	-
ke	zin	-	d	ga	-	ni	-	me	kya	-	r	he	-	ga	-
G	D	-	M	P	-	G	-	M	D	D	D	PD	N	P	-
te	ri	-	t	mn	-	na	-	ko	d	f	n	kr	-	ke	-
N	N	-	N	D	N	P	-	M*	M*	-	G	M*	P	P	-
te	re	-	kh	ya	-	lo	-	se	du	-	r	ja-	-	ke	-

flute: G- MDP- G S G--

G	D	-	M	P	-	G	-	M	M	D	D	PD	N	P	-
bu	jha	-	di	ye	-	hain	-	khud	a	p	ne	ha-	-	tho	-
-	N	N	N	D	N	P	-	M*	M*	-	G	M*	P	P	-
-	mo	h	bb	to	-	ke	-	di	ye	-	j	la	-	ke	-
G	D	-	M	P	-	G	-	M	D	-	P	PD	N	P	-
me	ri-	-	v	fa	-	ne	-	u	ja	-	d	di-	-	hai	-
N	N	-	N	D	N	P	-	M*	M*	-	G	M*	P	P	-
um	mi	-	d	ki	-	b	s	ti	ya	-	b	sa	-	ke	-

13. CHALE JA 3 JAHAAN PYAR MILE

Film: Jahaan Pyar Mile (1969) Music: Shanker Jaikishan
Lyrics: Hasrat Jaipuri Singer: Md. Rafi, Suman K.
Taal: Kaharwa dugun Chord: MDS' S=D

chale ja chale ja chale ja, jaha pyar mile, jaha pyar mile -3

itane bade jahan me koyi toh miit hoga
is gam ki bansuri me koyi toh giit hoga
chale ja chale ja chale ja...

chalana hi zindagi hai rukana hain maut teri
ae zindagi ke rahi kis baat ki hai deri
chale ja chale ja chale ja...

aawaz de rahi hai manzil tuje suhani
badhata hi chal musafir har saans ek kahaani
chale ja chale ja chale ja...

CHALE JA 3 JAHAAN PYAR MILE

dhage nti nke dhin	dhage nti nkedhin	dhagentinkedhin	dhagentinkedhin
12 34 56 78	12 34 56 78	12 3456 78	12 3456 78
prelude: R̲' S'---- M' ---- R̲'--- S'—M'-----			
S R̲ M P	D̲ S' N̲ D̲	D̲N̲ - - -	- - S' D̲
ch le ja ch	le ja ch le	ja- - - -	- - j ha
P M - M	M - S' D̲	P M - M	M - - -
pya - -r mi	le - j ha	pya - -r mi	le - - -
interlude:			

S'S'S' M'—M' S' R' S'
S'S'S' G'—G' S' R' N
NNN G'—G' R'- S'-
DDD R'—R' S'- N-
PPP S'—S' DPM--

				S'	S'
				i	t
S'R' G' R'G' -	R' S' - N	S' - S' -	- - S' -		
ne - - -	b de - j	ha - me -	- - ko -		
S'R' G' R'G' -	R' S' - N	S' - S' -	- - D	D	
ii - - -	to mi - t	ho - ga -	- - i	s	
D - - -	P D M M	DN R' R' -	- - R' -		
gm - - -	ki ba - su	ri- - me -	- - ko -		
S' - D -	M D - N	S' - S' -	- - - -		
ii - - -	to gi - t	ho - ga -	- - - -		

interlude: S'R'G' D'P'D'P' M'G'M'G' R'S'R'S' N-
              PDN M'G'M'G' R'S'R'S' ND PD S'-

				S'	S'
				ch	l
S'R' G' R'G' -	R' S' - N	S' - S' -	- - S'	S'
na - - -	hi zin - d	gi - hai -	- - ru	k
S'R' G' R'G' -	R' S' - N	S' - S' -	- - D -	
na - - -	hai mau - t	te - ri -	- - hai -	
D - - -	P D M M	DN R' R' -	- - R'	S'
zin - - -	d gi - ki	ra- - he -	- - ki	s
S' - D -	M D - N	S' - S' -	- - - -	
ba - - -	t ki - hai	de - ri -	- - - -	

14. CHURA LE NA TUMKO YE MAUSAM

Film: Dil hi to hai (1963)   Music: Roshan
Lyrics: Sahir Ludhiyanvi   Singer: Mukesh, Suman K.
Taal: Kaharwa   Chord: RGD RM*D   S=C

M: chura le na tum ko ye mausam suhaana
       khuli waadiyon men akeli na jaana
S: lubhaata hai mujhako ye mausam suhaana
       main jaaungi tum mere pichhe na aana

M: lipat jaaega koi bebaak jhonka
       jawaani ki rau men na anchal udaana
S: mere waaste tum pareshaa n hona
       mujhe khub ata hai daaman bachaana -2
       main jaaungi tum mere pichhe na aana

M: ghata bhi kabhi chum leti hai chehara
       samajh soch kar rukh se zulfen hataana
S: ghata mere nazadik aa ke to dekhe
       in ankhon ne sikha hai bijali giraana -2
       main jaaungi tum mere pichhe na aana

M: tum ek phool ho tumko dhundhunga kaise
       kahin milke phoolon mein gum ho na jaana
S: jo phoolon me rangat mile bhi to kya hai,
       juda meri khushbu juda muskurana -2
       main jaaungi tum mere pichhe na aana

CHURA LE NA TUMKO YE MAUSAM

dha	ge	n	ti	n	ke	dhi	n	dha	ge	n	ti	n	ke	dhi	n
1	2	3	4	5	6	7	8	1	2	3	4	5	6	7	8

prelude:
N G'- N G'- M*'P'M*'P' M*' G' M*'–
N M*'- N M*'- P'D'P'D' P' M*' G'-
D'-N'D' P'-D'P' M*'-P'M*' G'-
G GP ND ND G GP N-
Chord : (GPN)

1	2	3	4	5	6	7	8	1	2	3	4	5	6	7	8
														G	-
														chu	-
M*	-	-	R	-	G	-	M*	D	-	-	-	D	-	D	-
ra	-	-	-	-	le	-	n	tum	-	-	-	ko	-	ye	-
-	-	D	-	N	N	-	D	D	-	-	-	P	-	M*	-
-	-	mau	-	-	sm	-	su	ha	-	-	-	na	-	-	-
G	-	G	G	-	G	-	G	G	M*	-	-	G	-	R	-
-	-	khu	li	-	va	-	di	yon	-	-	-	me	-	-	-
R	-	M*	M*	-	P	-	M*	G	-	-	-	G	-	G	-
-	-	a	ke	-	li	-	n	ja	-	-	-	na	-	lu	-
M*	-	-	R	-	G	-	M*	D	-	D	-	D	-	D	-
bha	-	-	-	-	ta	-	hai	mu	-	jh	-	ko	-	ye	-
-	-	D	-	N	N	-	D	D	-	-	-	P	-	M*	-
-	-	mau	-	-	sm	-	su	ha	-	-	-	na	-	-	-
G	-	G	G	-	G	-	G	G	M*	-	-	G	-	R	-
-	-	main	ja	-	un	-	gi	tum	-	-	-	me	-	re	-
-	-	M*	-	-	P	-	M*	G	M*	G	-	G	-	-	-
-	-	pi	-	-	chhe	-	n	aa	-	-	-	na	-	-	-

antra:

		R'	R'	R'	N	-	R'	R'	-	D	-	D	-	D	-
		li	p	t	ja	-	ye	ga	-	-	-	ko	-	ii	-
-	-	R'	-	-	N	-	R'	R'	-	D	-	D	-	-	-
-	-	be	-	-	ba	-	q	jhau	-	-	-	ka	-	-	-
-	-	D	D	-	G	-	M*	N	-	-	-	N	-	N	-
-	-	j	va	-	ni	-	ki	rau	-	-	-	me	-	na	-
-	-	R'	-	-	N	-	N	D	-	-	-	D	-	R'	N
-	-	aan	-	-	chl	-	u	da	-	-	-	na	-	o	-
N	R'	R'	R'	-	N	-	R'	R'	-	D	-	D	-	-	-
o	-	me	re	-	va	-	s	te	-	-	-	tum	-	-	-
-	-	R'	R'	-	N	-	R'	R'	-	D	-	D	-	-	-
-	-	p	re	-	sha	-	n	ho	-	-	-	na	-	-	-
-	-	D	D	-	G	-	M*	N	-	-	-	N	-	N	-
-	-	mu	jhe	-	khu	-	b	aa	-	-	-	ta	-	hai	-
D	-	R'	-	-	N	-	N	D	-	-	-	D	-	G	-
-	-	da	-	-	mn	-	b	chha	-	-	-	na	-	mu	-
M*	-	-	R	-	G	-	M*	D	-	-	-	D	-	D	-
jhe	-	-	-	-	khu	-	b	aa	-	-	-	ta	-	hai	-
-	-	D	-	N	N	-	D	D	-	-	-	P	-	M*	-
-	-	da	-	-	mn	-	b	chha	-	-	-	na	-	-	-
G	-	G	G	-	G	-	G	G	M*	-	-	G	-	R	-
-	-	main	ja	-	un	-	gi	tum	-	-	-	me	-	re	-
-	-	M*	-	-	P	-	M*	G	M*	G	-	G	-	G	-
-	-	pi	-	-	chhe	-	n	aa	-	-	-	na	-	chu	-

M*	-	-	R	-	G	-	M*	D	-	-	-	D	-	D	-
ra	-	-	-	-	le	-	n	tum	-	-	-	ko	-	ye	-
-	-	D	-	N	N	-	D	D	-	-	-	P	-	M*	-
-	-	mau	-	-	sm	-	su	ha	-	-	-	na	-	-	-
G	-	G	G	-	G	-	G	G	M*	-	-	G	-	R	-
-	-	khu	li	-	va	-	di	yon	-	-	-	me	-	-	-
R	-	M*	M*	-	P	-	M*	G	-	-	-	G	-		
-	-	a	ke	-	li	-	n	ja	-	-	-	na	-		

15. CHHODO CHHODO MORI BAIYAAN

Film: Miyan Bivi Razi (1960) Music: Sachindev Burman
Lyrics: Shailendra Singer: Suman K.
Taal: Daadra Chord: RM*D S=C#

chodo chodo mori bainya sanwre
laj ke mare mai to pani pani hui jaun

nar naweli mai ganv ki gwalan janu na ye preet ki paheli
mohe dar lage -2 jhuth muth mai kahi badnam na ho jaun
chodo chodo mori bainya sanwre
o mitwa o mitwa

neer bharan ke roz bahane karun chori chori aau tose milne
tujhse nit jane kya -2 kya kahne ko aau bin kahe chali jau
chodo chodo mori bainya sanwre

aaj nahi to kal bhed khulega tab aate jate dunia degi tane
more man bhaye -2 kahe tohe dil diya mai badi pachtaun
chodo chodo mori bainya sanwre

CHHODO CHHODO MORI BAIYAAN

dha	dhi	na	dha	tun	na	dha	dhi	na	dha	tun	na
1	2	3	4	5	6	1	2	3	4	5	6
									D	<u>N</u>	-
									chho	do	-
P	-	D	P	M*	-	P	-	-	D	-	-
chho	-	do	mo	ri	-	bai	-	-	ya	-	-
-	-	ˢ'R'	-	-	<u>N</u>	D	-	-	-	-	-
-	-	saan-	-	-	v	re	-	-	-	-	-
D	-	D	S'	S'	-	R'	-	R'	<u>G</u>'	R'	-
la	-j	ke	ma	re	-	main	-	to	pa	ni	-
N	-	N	S'	R'	-	<u>N</u>	-	D	D	<u>N</u>	-
pa	-	ni	hu	ii	-	ja	-	un	chho	do	-
-	-	P	D	P	M*	P	-	-	D	-	-
-	-	chho	do	mo	ri	bai	-	-	ya	-	-
-	-	ˢ'R'	-	-	<u>N</u>	D	-	-	-	-	-
-	-	saan	-	-	v	re	-	-	-	-	-

interlude: DDR'<u>R</u>'R' DDS'NS'   DDS'-<u>N</u>-D-
DDD<u>N</u>- S'- R'<u>G</u>'R'--- S'- <u>N</u>D---

dha	dhi	na	dha	tun	na	dha	dhi	na	dha	tun	na
D	-	<u>N</u>	-	D	-	P	-	P	M*	G	-
na	-	r	-	n	-	ve	-	li	main	-	-
-	-	G	-	M*	-	P	-	-	D	-	-
-	-	gan	v	ki	-	gva	-	-	ln	-	-
D	-	R'	<u>R</u>'	R'	-	S'	-	N	S'	-	R'
ja	-	nu	n	hin	-	pri	-	t	ki	-	p

N	-	-	D	-	-	-	-	-	D	D	-
he	-	-	li	-	-	-	-	-	mo	he	-
D	-	-	S'	-	-	R'	-	-	-	-	-
d	r	-	la	-	-	ge	-	-	-	-	-
S'R'	-	-	N	-	-	D	-	-	D	D	-
-	-	-	-	-	-	-	-	-	mo	he	-
D	-	-	S'	-	-	R'	-	-	-	-	-
d	r	-	la	-	-	ge	-	-	-	-	-
D	-	D	S'	-	S'	R'	-	R'	G'	R'	R'
jhu	-	th	mu	-	th	main	-	k	hin	b	d
N	-	N	S'	R'	-	N	-	D	D	N	-
na	-	m	na	ho	-	ja	-	un	chho	do	-
N	-	P	D	P	M*	P	-	-	D	-	-
o	-	chho	do	mo	ri	bai	-	-	ya	-	-
-	-	S'R'	-	-	N	D	-	-	-	-	-
-	-	saan	-	-	v	re	-	-	-	-	-

D--- NG'R'----   N---- DPR---
o—   mitva----   o----mitva—

interlude:2   R ^{P}D—NG'R'---   NPN---   DPR---

DN DPP   M*G G   M*PP DD
nir bhrn   ke-   roz   bhane kru

DR'   R'R'   NN   S'R'   N D
chori   chori   aaun   tose   milne

DD   DD   S'S'   S'R'--- S'N---D
tose   nit   jane   kya-----------

```
DD    DD  S'S'  R'   DDS'  S'    R'R'
tose  nit jane  kya  khne  ko    aaun


G'R'   NN  S'R'   ND
bina   khe chli   jaun


DN    N   PD     PM*    PD       S'R'  N D
chhodo o chhodo  mori  baiyan  saan  v  re...
play rest song as above.
```

16. DAGABAZI PIYA TERE DIL ME HAI

Film: Aulad (1968)
Lyrics: Majrooh Sultanpuri
Taal: Kaharwa dugun

Music: Chitragupta
Singer: Suman K.
Chord: GM*N SGP S=C#

dil dhadkta hai paanv rukte hai dekhte log ye kis nazar se mujhe

dagabazi piya tere dil me hai -2

tera dil mere gaalo ke til me hai -2 til me hai til me hai

dagabazi piya tere dil me hai -2

tere naino ka uthna haye re mera anchal sarkata jaye re -2

mera uljhe hai man, kanpe hai tan, payal badi, mushkil me hai

dagabazi piya tere dil me hai -2

yahan lali uchhalti shishe me pariyan hain machalti shishe me -2

sab ko chodkar, teri nazar, mujhpe hi kyun, mehfil me hai

dagabazi piya tere dil me hai -2

pehle tum kalaiyaan, thamoge, fir gauri ye baaiyan, thamoge

sab janu balam teri kasam kya kya nahi, tere dil me hai

dagabazi piya tere dil me hai -2

DAGABAZI PIYA TERE DIL ME HAI

dhage	nti	nke dhin	dhage	nti	nke dhin	dhage	nti	nke dhin	dhage	nti	nke dhin
12	34	56 78	12	34	56 78	12	34	56 78	12	34	56 78

prelude:

PNR'S'NPN—PN—R'S'DN—

P-MGM P-MGM S'-NDS' S'-NDS'

M'M' M'M' M'M' M'R'S'

R'R' R'R' R'R' G'R'N

R'S'R'NS'D S'NS'DNM*D- M*N—

N --- S'NDP   D—S'NP--

aa----aa---   aa----------

P   PPMP P   PP PMN   N   S'DP   M   M SR GP M GG

dil dhdkta hai pav rukte   hain, dekhte log, ye kis nzr se mujhe

| | | | | | | | | | M* | M |
| | | | | | | | | | d | ga |

| G | -S | - | R | G | - | G | G | - | P | - | D | M* | | P | D |
| ba | -ji | - | pi | ya | - | te | re | - | dil | - | me | hai | - | te | ra |

| N | - | N | N | NS' | R' | S' | N | - | P | - | D | M* | - | P | D |
| dil | - | me | re | ga- | - | lo | ke | - | til | - | me | hai | - | te | ra |

| N | - | N | N | NS' | R' | R' | R' | S' | G' | - | R' | S' | R' | - | S' |
| dil | - | me | re | ga- | - | lo | ke | - | til | - | me | hai | til | - | me |

| N | N | - | D | M* | - | M* | M | GM | -S | - | R | G | - | G | G |
| hai | til | - | me | hai | - | d | ga | ba- | -ji | - | pi | ya | - | te | re |

| - | P | - | D | M* | - | M* | M | GM | -S | - | R | GM | P | M | S |
| - | dil | - | me | hai | - | d | ga | ba- | -ji | - | pi | ya- | - | te | re |

-	M	-	G	G	-		
-	dil	-	me	hai	-		

interlude:

PD<u>N</u>—R'—S'— PD<u>N</u> – S'—<u>N</u>— G'- S'- <u>R</u>'- N- PD<u>N</u> – S'—<u>N</u>-

S<u>RG</u>MP<u>D</u> <u>N</u>S'M'<u>G</u>' <u>N</u>S'M'<u>G</u>' <u>G</u>'<u>G</u>'<u>G</u>'<u>G</u>'

<u>D</u>NR'S' <u>N</u><u>R</u>'S' S'S'S'S'

M'<u>G</u>'<u>R</u>' S'<u>ND</u> M*M<u>R</u> S S<u>RG</u>MP<u>DN</u>—

						<u>N</u>	<u>N</u>
						te	re

<u>N</u>	-M*	-	M*	M	M*	<u>G</u>	-	-	M*	-	M*	M	-	M	M*
nai	-no	-	ka	u	th	na	-	-	ha	-	ye	re	-	me	ra

<u>N</u>	-<u>N</u>	-	<u>N</u>	S'	S'	P	<u>D</u>	<u>R</u>'	-	S'	-	<u>N</u>	*	<u>D</u>	<u>N</u>
aan	-ch	-l	s	r	k	ta	-	ja	-	ye	-	re	-	me	ra

R'	-R'	-	<u>G</u>'	S'	-	<u>D</u>	<u>N</u>	R'	-R'	-	<u>G</u>'	S'	-	<u>D</u>	<u>N</u>
ul	-jhe	-	hai	mn	-	-	-	kan	-pe	-	hai	tn	-	-	-

<u>R</u>'	-<u>R</u>'	-	S'	<u>G</u>'	-	-	S'	S'	<u>N</u>	-	<u>D</u>	M*	-		
pa	-y	-l	b	di	-	-	mu	sh	kil	-	me	hai	-		

interlude:

PD<u>N</u>—R'—S'-- PD<u>N</u>—S'—<u>N</u>—

<u>G</u>'—S'—<u>R</u>'—<u>N</u>-- PD<u>N</u>—S'—<u>N</u>—

S<u>RG</u>MP<u>D</u> <u>N</u>S'M'<u>G</u>' <u>N</u>S'M'<u>G</u>' <u>G</u>' <u>G</u>' <u>G</u>' <u>G</u>'

<u>D</u>NR'S' <u>N</u><u>R</u>'S' S' S' S' S'

M'<u>G</u>'<u>R</u>' S'<u>ND</u> M*M<u>R</u>S S<u>RG</u>MP<u>DN</u>—

						<u>N</u>	<u>N</u>
						y	ha

<u>N</u>	-M*	-	M*	M	M*	<u>G</u>	-	-	M*	-	M*	M	-	M	M*
la	-li	-	u	chh	l	ti	-	-	shi	-	she	me	-	p	ri

<u>N</u>	-<u>N</u>	-	<u>N</u>	S'	-	P	<u>D</u>	<u>R</u>'	-	S'	-	<u>N</u>	*	<u>D</u>	<u>N</u>
ya	-hain	-	m	chl	-	ti	-	shi	-	she	-	me	-	s	b

R'	-R'	-	G'	S'	-	D	N	R'	-R'	-	G'	S'	-	D	N
ko	-chho	-	d	kr	-	-	-	te	-ri	-	n	zr	-	-	-

R'	-R'	-	S'	G'	-	-	S'	S'	N	-	D	M*	-
mujh	-pe	-	hi	kyu	-	-	m	h	fi	-l	me	hai	-

NNN M* M*MM*G M*M*M MM* NN N S'PD R'S'N
phle tum klai-ya, thamoge, fir gori ye baiya- thamoge

DN R'R' G' S' DN R'R' G' S'DN R' R' S'G' S'S' N D M*
sb janu blm -- teri ksm -- kya kya nhin, tere dil me hai

M*M MS R G GG P D M*
dgabazi piya tere dil me hai

M*M MS R GMP MS M G G
dgabazi piya--- tere dil me hai

* M* N R' S'R' – S'R'-- S'R'N- M*DN--

17. DIN HO YA RAAT HAM RAHEIN

Film: Miss Bombay (1957)   Music: Hansraj Bahal
Lyrics: Prem Dhawan   Singer: Md. Rafi, Suman K.
Taal: Kaharwa dugun   Chord: SGP   S=E

din ho yaa raat ham rahen tere saath yah hamaari marzi
tumhaari marazi…. ji hamaari marzi…
tumhaari to hamaari bhi yahi hai marzi
din ho yaa raat …

too dor main patang udoon tere sang sang
ho ho ho ho ho ho aa ha ha ha ha
too hai phool to main rang rahoon tere sang sang
ho ho ho hu hu hu ho ho, ho ho ho
rang daalo is rang mein hamaara ang ang -2
ye tumhaari marazi… ji hamaari marzi…
tumhaari to hamaari bhi yahi hai marzi
din ho yaa raat …

le ke aaoon main baraat thamun mehandi wale haath
ho ho ho ho ho ho aa ha ha ha ha
main to mukh se na boloon chali chaloon tere saath
ho ho ho hu hu hu ho ho, ho ho ho
nit nit kare chanda se chakori mulaaqaat -2
ye tumhaari marazi… ji hamaari marzi…
tumhaari to hamaari bhi yahi hai marzi
din ho yaa raat …

ik bangalaa ho pyaara saari duniya se nyara

ho ho ho ho ho ho aa ha ha ha ha

jisaki chaandi ki diwaaren aur sone ka dwara

ho ho ho hu hu hu ho ho, ho ho ho

jiske angana mein aake bhool jaaoon jag sara -2

ye tumhaari marazi... ji hamaari marzi...

tumhaari to hamaari bhi yahi hai marzi

din ho yaa raat ...

DIN HO YA RAAT HAM RAHEIN

dhage nti	nke	dhin	dhage	nti	nke dhin	dhage nti	nke dhin	dhage	nti	nke dhin
12 34	56	78	12	34	56 78	12 34	56 78	12	34	56 78

S'S'S'S'S' <u>N</u> D P M G R S
ho--------------------------

S   S   R   P   P   P P   S   S R   P   P   P   P
ho ho ho   ho ho ho ho   ho ho ho   ho ho ho ho

S   S   S   .<u>N</u> | .<u>N</u> SS .<u>N</u> .P | S   S   S .<u>N</u> | .<u>N</u> SS .<u>N</u> .P
di n   ho ya | ra -t h   m | r   he te re | sa -th ye h

.<u>N</u> .<u>N</u> S   R | S   -   -   P | P   P S' S' | <u>N</u>S' - S' P
ma ri m   r | zi -   - tum | ha ri m   r | zi - ji h

P   PS' N   D | P   -   -   P | P   S' <u>N</u> D | P   P   M   M
ma ri- m   r | zi -   - tum | ha ri to h | ma ri bhi y

G   G   R   S | RG MG R   -
hi hai m   r | zi- -   -   -
interlude:
P <u>N</u> NS'S' S' <u>N</u>S' -2
P <u>N</u> S'R'R'- R' R'-------- R'--- R'---- R'S'-----

```
                                                    P   N
                                                    tu  -

S'  -S'  S'   N  | N   S'  P   N  | S'  S'  S'  N  | N   S'  P   N
do  -r   main p  | tn  g   u   du | te  re  sn  g  | sn  g   ho  ho

S'  -    P    N  | S'  -   P   N  | R'  -   S'  -  | S'  -   P   N
ho  -    ho   ho | ho  -   ha  ha | ha  -   ha  -  | ha  -   tu  hai

S'  -S'  S'   N  | N   S'  P   N  | S'  S'  S'  N  | N   S'  P   N
fu  -l   to   main| rn g   r   hu | te  re  sn  g  | sn  g   ho  ho

S'  -    P    N  | S'  -   P   N  | R'  -   S'  -  | S'  -   P   D
ho  -    ho   ho | ho  -   ha  ha | ha  -   ha  -  | ha  -   rn  g

N   N    D    P  | D   D   P   R  | S   N   S   R  | S   S   P   P
da  ro   i    s  | rn  g   me  h  | ma  ra  an  g  | an  g   ye  tum

P   P    S'   S' | N   S'  S'  P  | P   PS' N   D  | P   -   -   P
ha  ri   m    r  | zi  -   ji  h  | ma  ri- m   r  | zi  -   -   tum

P   S'   N    D  | P   P   M   M  | G   G   R   S  | RG  MG  R   -
ha  ri   to   h  | ma  ri  bhi y  | hi  hai m   r  | zi  -   -   -
```

interlude:

P N NS'S' S' NS' -2

P N S'R'R'- R' R'-------- R'--- R'---- R'S'-----

```
PN      S'S'    S'      NS'S'      PN        S'  S'   S'N     S'S'
leke    aaun    main    barat,     thamu     mehndi  vale     ha  th

P N  S'  –       P N  S' -         P N  R' – S'- S'-
hohoho-     hohoho-           ha ha ha – ha- ha-

P       N    S'S'     S'  N   S'S'    PN   S'S'   S'N      S'S'
main    to   mukh     se  na  bolu,   chli chlu   tere     Sth
```

```
P N S' –    P N S' -      P N R' – S'- S'-
hohoho-   hohoho-      ha ha ha – ha- ha-


PD NN DP DD    P RS.N    SRSS
nit-nit  kre chnda  se chkori  mulakat  -2


P    PPP    S'S'S'    S' PPS'  NDP
ye  tumhari  mrji--   ji hmari  mrji--


PPS'     N DPP  M  MG G  RS RG MG R -
tumhari  to hmari bhi  yhi hai Mr ji--------
```

18.   DIL EK MANDIR HAI

Film: Dil Ek Mandir (1963)   Music: Shanker Jaikishan
Lyrics: Hasrat Jaipuri   Singer: Md. Rafi, Suman K.
Taal: Daadra   Chord: MDS' S=D

jaanewaale kabhi nahin ate, jaanewaalon ki yaad ati hai

dil ek mndir hai, dil ek mndir hai -2

pyaar ki jis men hoti hai puja, ye pritam ka ghar hai

dil ek mndir hai, dil ek mndir hai -2

har dhadkan hai arati wndan, ankh jo michi ho ge darshan -2

maut mita de chaahe hasti, yaad to amar hai -2

ham yaadon ke ful chadhaayein, aur ansu ke dip jalaayein -2

saanson ka har taar pukaare ye prem nagar hai -2

DIL EK MANDIR HAI

dha	tin	tin	ta	dhin	dhin	dha	tin	tin	ta	dhin	dhin
1	2	3	4	5	6	1	2	3	4	5	6

S M D̲ R' S'   D̲ M S'
aa----------   aa-----

S'R̲' S'R̲'--------   S'S'R̲'G'   R'R'   S'S'--
jane vale--------   kbhi----- nhin aate---,

N̲N̲ N̲N̲ N̲ N̲D̲D̲ P—M   M
jane vale ki ya-d aa--ti   hai

SR	RM	-M	P	D̲	D̲	P	-	-	-	D̲	M
dil	e-	-k	mn	di	r	hai	-	-	-	-	-

MP	PS'	-S'	S'	G'	R̲'	S'	-	-	-	-	-
dil	e-	-k	mn	di	r	hai	-	-	-	-	-

N̲D	-	D̲,D̲	PD̲	P	M	D̲	D̲	D̲	PD̲	P	-M
pya	-	r,ki	jis	me	-	ho	ti	hai	pu-	ja	-ye

P	D̲	-P	M	M	-R̲	S	-	-	-	-	-
pri	t	-m	ka	gh	-r	hai	-	-	-	-	-

SR	RM	-M	P	D̲	D̲	P	-	-	-	D̲	M
dil	e-	-k	mn	di	r	hai	-	-	-	-	-

MP	PS'	-S'	S'	G'	R̲'	S'	-	-	-	-	-
dil	e-	-k	mn	di	r	hai	-	-	-	-	-

interlude:

D̲NS'R̲'M'---

G'M' G'M' G'M' G'M' P'M'G'S' P'—

M'P' M'P' M'P' M'P' D̲'P'M'R̲' P'—

S' M' G'---- R̲' S' --- N̲ D

M R̲'S' N̲D PM--

M	M	M	M	M	G	M	P	M	R̲	S	-
hr	dh	d	kn	hai	-	aa	r	ti	vn	dn	-

P	P	P	P	P	M	D̲	D̲	D̲	PD̲	P	M
aan	kh	jo	mi	chi	-	ho	g	ye	dr	shn	-

D̲	D̲	D̲	D̲	D̲	M	D̲	S'	-	S'	S'	-
mau	t	mi	ta	de	-	chha	he	-	h	sti	-

R̲'	R̲'	R̲'	R̲'	R̲'	R̲'	S'	-	-	-	-	-
ya	d	to	a	m	r	hai	-	-	-	-	-

interlude:

MPD̲-P- MPD̲-P-
R̲GM-G- R̲GM-G̲-
.NSR̲-S- .NSR̲-S-
.M.P.D̲-.P- M—

M	M	-	M	M	G	P	P	M	R̲	S	-
hm	ya	-	do	ke	-	fu	l	ch	dha	yen	-

P	P	-	P	P	M	D̲	D̲	D̲	PD̲	P	M
aur	aan	-	su	ke	-	di	p	j	la-	yen	-

D̲	D̲	-	D̲	M	D̲	S'	S'	S'	S'	S'	S'
san	so	-	ka	h	r	ta	r	pu	ka	re	ye

R̲'	-	R̲'	R̲'	R̲'	R̲'	S'	-	-	-	-	-
pre	-	m	n	g	r	hai	-	-	-	-	-

19. DIL KI KITAB KORI HAI

Film: Yaar Mera (1971)　　　　Music: Shanker Jaikishan
Lyrics: Hasrat Jaipuri　　　　Singer: Suman K., Md. Rafi
Taal: Kaharwa dugun　　　　Chord: PNR' S=C

ho dil ki kitab kori hai, kori hi rahne do -2
haaye jo ab tak chhori hai chhori hi rahne do
dil ko churana chori hai chori hi rahne do
agar ye zora zori hai zori hi rahne do

chnda ko lage grahan suraj ko lage grahan -2
chnda ko lage suraj ko lage, lagne do lage grahan
haye pyar ki chandani gori hai, gori hi rahne do
ho dil ki kitab kori hai, kori hi rahne do

jab phul koi khil jaye lahraake bhawra aaye -2
aane do agar aata hai idhar, phir apne aap ud jaye
harjayi ye aadat tori hai, tori hi rahne do
ho dil ki kitab kori hai, kori hi rahne do

chal doge muskuraake, nazro se tum girake -2
jab pyar kiya iqrar kiya, manenge ham nibhake
haay teri meri ye jodi hai jodi hi rahne do
ho dil ki kitab kori hai, kori hi rahne do

DIL KI KITAB KORI HAI

dhage	nti	nke	dhin	dhage	nti	nke	dhin	dhage	nti	nke	dhin	dhage	nti	nke	dhin
12	34	56	78	12	34	56	78	12	34	56	78	12	34	56	78
															N
															o
N	N	DN	-P	P	DN	N	D	G	PS′	-	S′	N	D	P	-
dil	ki	kita	-b	ko	ri-	hai	-	ko	ri-	-	hi	rh	ne	do	-
N	-N	DN	DP	P	DN	N	D	G	PS′	-	S′	N	D	P	-
ha	y,jo	ab	tk	chho	ri-	hai	-	chho	ri-	-	hi	rh	ne	do	-
N	NN	DN	DP	P	DN	N	D	G	PS′	-	S′	N	D	P	-
dil	ko,chu	ra-	na	cho	ri-	hai	-	cho	ri-	-	hi	rh	ne	do	-
N	N	DN	DP	P	DN	N	D	G	PS′	-	S′	N	D	P	-
gr	ye	zo-	ra	zo	ri-	hai	-	zo	ri-	-	hi	rh	ne	do	-

interlude:

G′—R′ N R′ R′ N R′ G′—R′ N R′ R′ N R′ G′—R′ N R′ R′ N R′

R′ R′ G′ G′ M′ P′ G′

D′- D′ - P′ G′ G′ R′ D′- D′ - P′ G′ G′ R′

DD NN S′S′ R′R′ G′—P--

dhage	nti	nke	dhin	dhage	nti	nke	dhin	dhage	nti	nke	dhin	dhage	nti	nke	dhin
															R′
															chn
R′	R′	R′R′	-G′	G′	-	-	S′	S′	S′	DD	-R′	R′	-	-	G′
da	ko	lge	-gr	hn	-	-	su	rj	ko	lge	-gr	hn	-	-	chn
G′	G′R′	S′	G′	G′	G′R′	S′	S′S′	S′	S′	DD	-R′	R′	-	-	N
da	ko,l	ge	su	rj	ko,l	ge	lg	ne	do	lge	-gr	hn	-	-	hay
N	NN	D	NP	P	DN	N	D	G	PD	-	S′	N	D	P	-
pya	r,ki	chan	dni	go	ri-	hai	-	go	ri-	-	hi	rh	ne	do	-
															R′R′
															jb

R'	R'R'	R'R'R'G'	G'	G'	-	S'S'	S'	S'	D	DR'	R'	R'	-	G'
fu	l,ko	ii khil	ja	ye	-	lh	ra	ke	bhnv	ra-	aa	ye	-	aa

G'	G'R'	S'	G'	G'	G'R'	S'	S'	DD	ND	-R'	R'	R'	R'	-	N
ne	do,a	gr	aa	ta	hai,idhr	fir		ap	ne,aa	-p	ud	ja	ye	-	hr

N	N	D	PP	P	DN	N	D	G	PD	-	S'	N	D	P	-
ja	ii	aa	dt	to	ri-	hai	-	to	ri-	-	hi	rh	ne do	-	

20. DIL NE FIR YAAD KIYA

Film: Dil Ne Fir Yaad Kiya (1966)　　Music: Sonik Omi
Lyrics: G L Rawal　　Singer: Suman K., Md. Rafi,
Taal: Kaharwa　　Mukesh
　　Chord: SMD　S=C#

dil ne fir yaad kiya bark si lahar aai hai
fir koi chot mohobbat ki ubhar aai hai

wo bhi kya din the hamen dil men bithhaaya tha kabhi
aur hns hns ke gale tum ne lagaaya tha kabhi
khel hi khel men kyon jaan pe ban aayi hai

kya bataaye tumhen ham shamma ki kismat kya hai
gam men jalane ke siwa aur mohobbat kya hai
ye wo gulashan hai ke jisame na bahaar aai hai

ham wo parawaane hai jo shamma ka dam bharte hai
husn ki aag men khaamosh jala karte hai
ah bhi nikale to ye pyaar ki ruswaayi hai

DIL NE FIR YAAD KIYA

dha	ge	n	ti	n	ke	dhi	n	dha	ge	n	ti	n	ke	dhi	n
1	2	3	4	5	6	7	8	1	2	3	4	5	6	7	8

prelude:

D--- P M , D --- P M, M M S, S' N D PM PM

flute: NS' NS' NS' – N D P M G R S

 S R MP DN DPM PP   P MGM GRGR S

dil ne fir yad kiya brk sii lhra   ii...   hai

M M DN S'S' S'N S'N D PMP DP M- P-MGRS

dil ne fir yad kiya brk sii lhra ii...   hai

S RMP DN DPMPP   P PMG M GRGR S

fir koii- chot mohbbt ki ubhr aa ii...   hai

S R MP DN DPM

dil ne fir yad   kiya

Music: flute

S' --- G'R' M' – S'

G'R'N – R'R'G'R'M' – S'

R' --- S'NDPM – D –N S' R' – D

Synthe:

M G R --- S M G R --- S .N S R M S ---

S' R' S' N N DP D D MDNR'- N N   R'S'

vo bhi kya din the hme dil me bitha-ya-   tha kbhi

S' R' S'R' N N DP   D D MDNR'- N N   R'S'

vo bhi kya din the hme dil me bitha-ya-   tha kbhi

S'R' S'N R'R' R' R'S' G'---- R'   G'R'S' S' NS' DPM

aur hns hns ke gle tum---ne   lga- ya   tha- kbhi-

MM DN S'R' S'   N S'N D PM   P DP M- PMGRS
khel hi- khel   me kyu jan pe bn aa ii   hai -------

S   RMP DN   DPMPP   P PMG   M GRGR S
fir koii- chot mohbbt ki ubhr   aa ii...   hai

S   R MP DN DPM
dil ne fir   yad kiya

interlude:
M PM MN D --- D M
P DP P R' S' ---R' S'
G' M' – G' M' – G' M' –
flute: M P D P – R' S' D P S'--

S' R'S'-N   NS'   DP   DD   M DNR'R'N R' S'
kya bta-en tumhe   hm shmma ki kismt-   kya hai -2

S' R'S'R'N   NS'   DP DD   M DNR'R'N R' S'
kya bta-en   tumhe hm shmma ki kismt-   kya hai -2

S' R' S'NR' S' R'S'N G'--R' G'R'S'S'S' ᴺS'   D-- PM
gm me jlne   ke siva- au-r   moh-bbt kya   hai--

M M DNS'   S' S'   NNS' N DPM PMDP M- PMGRS
ye vo gulshn hai ke jisme n bhar aani   hai

S   RMP DN   DPMPP   P PMG   M GRGR S
fir koii- chot mohbbt ki ubhr   aa ii...   hai

S   R MP DN DPM
dil ne fir   yad kiya

P   D PMMM   PM GS   SG   M P   P D   PM
hm vo prvane   hai- jo- shmma ka dm bhrte   hain - - 2

```
N    D  PMMM  PM  GS    SG    M   P   PD    M
hm  vo  prvane  hai- jo- shmma  ka  dm bhrte  hain -2

DN    S'N  NN    N     S'R'S'R'--R'    S'NR'  S'----D  PM
husn ki-  aag   me  kha-mo---sh  jla-   kr---te  hain-

MM   DN  S'S'S' S' N    S'N  D   PMPMDP  M-  PMGRS
aah   bhi  nikle  to ye  pyar ki  rusva-ii-   hai -------
```

21.   GARJAT BARSAT SAAWAN AAYO

Film: Barsaat ki Raat (1960)   Music: Raushan

Lyrics: Sahir Ludhiyanvi   Singer: Kamal Barot, Sudha Malhotra, Suman K.

Taal: Teen Taal   Chord: GPS' RMD   S=C#

garajat barasat saawan ayo re -2

laayo n sng me hamre bichhade balamawa,

sakhi ka karun haay, garajat barasat saawan ayo re

garajat barasat saawan

ayo re, saawan ayo, saawan ayo re, garajat barasat saawan

rimajhim rimajhim meha barase, rimajhim rimajhim

meha – barase – barase -, meha

rimajhim rimajhim meha barase

tadape jiyarawa miin samaan

pad gayi fiki laal chunariya, piya nahin aaye

garajat barasat saawan ayo re garajat barasat saawan

pal-pal chhin-chhin pawan jhakore -3

laage tan par tir samaan, tir samaan, aa......

sakhi laage tan par tir samaan

nainan jal son bhigi chadariya, agan lagaae

garajat barasat saawan ayo re

laayo n sng me hamre bichhade balamawa

sakhi ka karun haay, garajat barasat saawan ayo –

laayo na – sang me – hamre – bhichhade – balamva,

sakhi ka karun haay re haay

GARJAT BARSAT SAAWAN AAYO

dha	dhin	dhin	dha	dha	dhin	dhin	dha	dha	tin	tin	ta	ta	dhin	dhin	dha
1	2	3	4	5	6	7	8	9	10	11	12	13	14	15	16
								R	R	P	P	P	P	M	P
								g	r	j	t	b	r	s	t
S'	–	D	P	G	P	M	–	R	R	P	P	P	P	M	P
sa	–	v	n	aa	yo	re	–	g	r	j	t	b	r	s	t
S'	–	D	P	G	P	M	–	M	N̲	D	P	G	P	M	–
sa	–	v	n	aa	yo	re	–	la	–	yo	re	sn	g	me	–
G	R	G	–	G	P	M	R	.N	R	S	–	–	–	M	G
h	m	re	–	bi	chh	de	b	l	m	va	–	–	–	s	khi
M	N̲	D	P	M	–	–	R	R	R	P	P	P	P	M	P
ka	–	k	ru	ha	–	–	y	g	r	j	t	b	r	s	t
S'	–	D	P	G	P	M	–	R	R	P	P	P	P	M	P
sa	–	v	n	aa	yo	re	–	g	r	j	t	b	r	s	t
S'	–	S'	S'	–	S'	S'	S'	G'	R'	G'	M'	R'	–	S'	–
sa	–	v	n	–	aa	yo	re	sa	–	v	n	aa	–	yo	–
–	S'	D	P	G	P	M	–	R	R	P	P	P	P	M	P
–	sa	v	n	aa	yo	re	–	g	r	j	t	b	r	s	t

S'	-	S'	S'	-	-	-	-								
sa	-	v	n	-	-	-	-								
P	P	P	P	P	P	S'	D	S'	-	S'	-	N	R'	S'	-
ri	m	jhi	m	ri	m	jhi	m	me	-	ha	-	b	r	se	-
P	P	P	P	P	P	S'	D	S'	-	S'	-	-	-	P	P
ri	m	jhi	m	ri	m	jhi	m	me	-	ha	-	-	-	b	r
S'	-	-	-	-	-	P	P	PD	N	-	-	N	-	M	P
se	-	-	-	-	-	b	r	se-	-	-	-	me	-	ha	-
P	P	P	P	P	P	S'	D	S'	-	S'	-	N	R'	S'	-
ri	m	jhi	m	ri	m	jhi	m	me	-	ha	-	b	r	se	-
D	D	D	D	S'	S'	S'	-	S'	-	S'	S'	D	-	P	P
t	r	pe	ji	y	r	va	-	mi	-	n	s	ma	-	-	n
R	R	P	P	P	-	M	P	S'	-	D	P	G	P	M	-
p	d	g	yi	fi	-	ki	-	la	-	l	chu	n	ri	ya	-
M	N	-D	P	M	-	-	R	R	R	P	P	P	P	M	P
pi	ya	-n	hin	aa	-	-	y	g	r	j	t	b	r	s	t
S'	-	S'	S'	-	-	-	-								
sa	-	v	n	-	-	-	-								
P	P	P	P	P	P	S'	D	S'	S'	S'	S'	N	R'	S'	-
p	l	p	l	chhi	n	chhi	n	p	v	n	jh	ko	-	re	-
D	D	M	P	N	D	M	P	S'	S'	S'	S'	N	R'	S'	-
p	l	p	l	chhi	n	chhi	n	p	v	n	jh	ko	-	re	-
P	P	P	P	P	P	S'	D	S'	S'	S'	S'	N	R'	S'	-
p	l	p	l	chhi	n	chhi	n	p	v	n	jh	ko	-	re	-

S'	G'	G'	M'	R'	R'	S'	S'	N	R'	S'	S'	D	-	P	P
la	-	ge	-	t	n	p	r	ti	-	r	s	ma	-	-	n
P	-	S'	D	S'	-	-	S'	S'D	PP	MM	PP	DD	S'-	S'	S'
ti	-	r	s	ma	-	-	n	aa-	--	--	--	--	-	s	khi
S'	G'	G'	M'	R'	R'	S'	S'	N	R'	S'	S'	D	-	P	P
la	-	ge	-	t	n	p	r	ti	-	r	s	ma	-	-	n
R	-	P	P	P	P	M	P	S'	-	D	P	G	P	M	-
nai	-	n	n	j	l	so	-	bhi	-	gi	ch	d	ri	ya	-
M	N	-D	P	M	-	-	R	R	R	P	P	P	P	M	P
a	g	-n	l	ga	-	-	y	g	r	j	t	b	r	s	t
S'	-	D	P	G	P	M	-	R	R	P	P	P	P	M	P
sa	-	v	n	aa	yo	re	-	g	r	j	t	b	r	s	t
S'	-	D	P	G	P	M	-	M	N	D	P	G	P	M	-
sa	-	v	n	aa	yo	re	-	la	-	yo	re	sn	g	me	-
G	R	G	-	G	P	M	R	.N	R	S	-	-	-	M	G
h	m	re	-	bi	chh	de	b	l	m	va	-	-	-	s	khi
M	N	D	P	M	-	-	R	R	R	P	P	P	P	M	P
ka	-	k	ru	ha	-	-	y	g	r	j	t	b	r	s	t
S'	-	D	P	G	P	M	-	R	R	P	P	P	P	M	P
sa	-	v	n	aa	yo	re	-	g	r	j	t	b	r	s	t
S'	-	S'	S'	-	S'	S'	S'	G'	R'	G'	M'	R'	-	S'	-
sa	-	v	n	-	aa	yo	re	sa	-	v	n	aa	-	yo	
-	S'	D	P	G	P	M	-	R	R	P	P	P	P	M	P
-	sa	v	n	aa	yo	re	-	g	r	j	t	b	r	s	t

G'	-	-	R'	S'	N	R'	S'	x	DS'	R'	S'	D	-	P	-
sa	-	-	v	n	aa	-	yo	x	la-	-	yo	na	-	-	-
x	S'	N	S'	x	<u>N</u>	D	<u>N</u>	x	D	P	D	x	P	M	D
x	sn	g	me	x	h	m	re	x	bi	chh	de	x	b	l	m
MD	PM	GR	S-	M	P	M	P	D	<u>N</u>	-	<u>N</u>	-	D	M	P
va-	--	--	--	s	khi	ka	-	k	ru	-	ha	-	y	re	-
S'	-	-	-												
ha	-	-	y												

22.   HAMNE MANA HAMPE SAJAN

Film: Dada (1979)
Lyrics: Mahendra Dehlavi
Taal: Kaharwa

Music: Usha Khanna
Singer: Suman K.
Chord: GPS'   S=C#

humne mana hum pe sajan jobanva bharpur hai -2
ye to mahima ram ki ie me hamra ka kasur hai -2

saal solva laga humko ye to hum bhi janat hai
hamari bagiya mehake phulwa ye to hum bhi manat hai
chingari se aag bhaye ham sach ye baat zarur hai -2
ye to mahima ram ki ie me hamra ka kasur hai -2

daar ke kazra khaa ke gilaori hum jis aur nikal jaye
than jaaye hai diwano me chakku chhuriyaa chal jaye
sara shehar hai aashiq hamra hamka bahut garur hai -2
ye to mahima ram ki ie me hamra ka kasur hai -2

pehle gaona karvaiyenge fir sun meethi batiyaan
sabka thenga dikhlaai ke rang deihai tohri satiyaan
ab hu paas na aao hamre ab hu dilli dur hai -2
ye to mahima ram ki ie me hamra ka kasur hai -2
humne mana hum pe sajan jobanva bharpur hai -2
ye to mahima ram ki ie me hamra ka kasur hai -2

HAMNE MANA HAMPE SAJAN

dha	ge	n	ti	n	ke	dhi	n	dha	ge	n	ti	n	ke	dhi	n
1	2	3	4	5	6	7	8	1	2	3	4	5	6	7	8

prelude:
PDS'R'G' PDG'R'S' PDS'R' G'- R'S' R'- S'- S'- ND N- D-
N- DP D- P- DNS' NDP GRS

	S'	-	S'	S'	-	S'[R']	-	N	-	N	S'	D	-	D	P
	hm	-	ne	ma	-	na	-	hm	-	pe	-	sa	-	j	n
P	-	D	D	P	-	M	M	P	-	-	P	N	D	S'	-
jo	-	b	n	va	-	bh	r	pu	-	-	r	hai	-	-	-
-	S'	-	S'	S'	-	S'[R']	-	N	-	N	S'	D	-	D	P
-	hm	-	ne	ma	-	na	-	hm	-	pe	-	sa	-	j	n
P	-	D	D	P	-	M	M	P	-	-	M	G	R	S	-
jo	-	b	n	va	-	bh	r	pu	-	-	r	hai	-	-	-
-	G	-	G	G	R	R	G	G	S	-	S	S	-	P	P
-	ye	-	to	m	hi	ma	-	ra	-	-	m	ki	-	i	ma
P	D	D	S'	-	S'	-	N	D	-	-	P	P	-	-	-
h	m	ra	-	-	ka	-	k	su	-	-	r	hai	-	-	-
-	G	-	G	G	R	R	G	G	S	-	S	S	-	P	P
-	ye	-	to	m	hi	ma	-	ra	-	-	m	ki	-	i	ma
P	D	D	S'	-	S'	-	N	D	-	-	P	P	-	-	-
h	m	ra	-	-	ka	-	k	su	-	-	r	hai	-	-	-

interlude: P – D R' S' – N D   P – D R' S' – N N
D – N G' G̲' – R' S'   [D]S' R'G̲'R'G̲' S'---

S'	-	S'	R'	-	R'	G'	-	G'	-	G'	-	G'	-	G'	-
sa	-	l	so	-	l	va	-	la	-	ga	-	h	m	ko	-

S'	-	S'	-	R'	-	G'	-	S'	-	S'	S'	S'	-	-	-
ye	-	to	-	h	m	bhi	-	ja	-	n	t	hain	-	-	-
S'	S'	R'	-	R'	R'	R'	-	R'	R'	R'	-	R'	R'	R'	-
h	m	ri	-	b	gi	ya	-	m	h	ke	-	fu	l	va	-
N	-	N	-	D	-	N	-	P	-	P	P	P	PG'R'D'	S'-	
ye	-	to	-	h	m	bhi	-	ma	-	n	t	hain	-	-	-
S'	-	S'	-	S'	-	S'	-	N	-	N	S'	N	-	D	-
chin	-	ga	-	ri	-	se	-	aa	-	g	bh	ye	-	h	m
P	P	D	-	P	-	M	M	P	-	-	P	N	D	S'	-
s	ch	ye	-	ba	-	t	z	ru	-	-	r	hai	-	-	-
S'	-	S'	-	S'	-	S'	-	N	-	N	S'	N	-	D	-
chin	-	ga	-	ri	-	se	-	aa	-	g	bh	ye	-	h	m
P	P	D	-	P	-	M	M	P	-	-	M	G	R	S	-
s	ch	ye	-	ba	-	t	z	ru	-	-	r	hai	-	-	-
-	G	-	G	G	R	R	G	G	S	-	S	S	-	P	P
-	ye	-	to	m	hi	ma	-	ra	-	-	m	ki	-	i	ma
P	D	D	S'	-	S'	-	N	D	-	-	P	P	-	-	-
h	m	ra	-	-	ka	-	k	su	-	-	r	hai	-	-	-
-	G	-	G	G	R	R	G	G	S	-	S	S	-	P	P
-	ye	-	to	m	hi	ma	-	ra	-	-	m	ki	-	i	ma
P	D	D	S'	-	S'	-	N	D	-	-	P	P	-		
h	m	ra	-	-	ka	-	k	su	-	-	r	hai	-		

interlude:

P – D R' S' – N D   P – D R' S' – N N
D – N G' G̱' – R' S'   ᴰS' R'G̱'R'G̱' S'---

S'	-	S'	S'	R'	R'	G'	-	G'	-	G'	G'	G'	-	G'	-
da	-	r	ke	k	j	ra	-	kha	-	ke	gi	lau	-	ri	-
S'	-	S'	S'	R'	-	G'	G'	S'	-	S'	S'	S'	-	-	-
h	m	ji	s	o	-	r	ni	kl	-	ja	-	yen	-	-	-
S'	-	R'	-	R'	-	R'	-	R'	-	R'	-	R'	-	R'	-
thn	-	ja	-	ye	-	hai	-	di	-	va	-	no	-	me	-
N	-	N	-	D	N	N	-	P	-	P	-	P	PG'R'D'	S'-	
ch	k	ku	-	chhu	ri	ya	-	chl	-	ja	-	yen	-	-	-
S'	-	S'	S'	S'	S'	S'	-	N	-	N	S'	N	D	D	-
sa	-	ra	sh	h	r	hai	-	aa	-	shi	k	h	m	ra	-
P	P	D	-	P	P	M	M	P	-	-	P	N	D	S'	-
h	m	ka	-	b	hu	t	g	ru	-	-	r	hai	-	-	-
S'	-	S'	S'	S'	S'	S'	-	N	-	N	S'	N	D	D	-
sa	-	ra	sh	h	r	hai	-	aa	-	shi	k	h	m	ra	-
P	P	D	-	P	P	M	M	P	-	-	M	G	R	S	-
h	m	ka	-	b	hu	t	g	ru	-	-	r	hai	-	-	-
-	G	-	G	G	R	R	G	G	S	-	S	S	-	P	P
-	ye	-	to	m	hi	ma	-	ra	-	-	m	ki	-	i	ma
P	D	D	S'	-	S'	-	N	D	-	-	P	P	-	-	-
h	m	ra	-	-	ka	-	k	su	-	-	r	hai	-	-	-

23.   HAAN, MAINE BHI PYAR KIYA

Film: Boond Jo Ban Gayi Moti (1967)   Music: Satish Bhatia
Lyrics: Bharat Vyas   Singer: Mukesh, Suman K.
Taal: Kaharwa   Chord: RMD   S=D

M: haan, maine bhi pyaar kiya, pyaar se kab inkaar kiya
          bhigi bhigi raate, mithhi mithhi baaten
          aur maine dil ko nisaar kiya, haan,

S: maine bhi pyaar kiya

M: pyaar se kab inkaar kiya

S: pyaar se kab inkaar kiya
          bhigi bhigi raate, mithhi mithhi baaten
          aur maine dil ko nisaar kiya,

M: haan, maine bhi pyaar kiya

M: pyaar kiya kaliyon ke mahakate angon se
          pyaar kiya maine gul ke gulaabi gaalon se

S: aa ha ha aa ha ha aa
          pyaar kiya nargis ki nashili ankhon se
          pyaar kiya badali ki rngili zulfon se
          khuli chaandani men aa haa haa
          khuli chaandani men maine abhisaar kiya

B: haan, maine bhi pyaar kiya

M: thaam liya siine pe uchhalti laharon ko
          jhum uthha baahon men pakad tufaanon ko

S: aa ha ha aa ha ha aa

M: chum liya bijali se machalate hothhon ko
          lut liya maine mast ubharti bahaaron ko
          raat ki dulhan ka

S: aa ha ha

M: raat ki dulhan ka maine singaar kiya

B: haan, maine bhi pyaar kiya

HAAN, MAINE BHI PYAR KIYA

dha	ge	n	ti	n	ke	dhi	n	dha	ge	n	ti	n	ke	dhi	n
1	2	3	4	5	6	7	8	1	2	3	4	5	6	7	8

prelude:

flute: D--- NS'R'- D— ND DP PM

Synthe: RR MR RR PR RR PR RD RM DD S'D DR'S'N D-

piyano: R' S' D P, M G R S .D

1	2	3	4	5	6	7	8	1	2	3	4	5	6	7	8
						M	-	-	-	M	-	G	-	S	-
						ha	-	-	-	main	-	ne	-	bhi	-
R	-	R	R	R	-	-	-	M	-	M	M	G	G	S	S
pya	-	r	ki	ya	-	-	-	pya	-	r	se	k	b	i	n
R	-	R	R	R	-	-	-	P	P	P	P	D	-	P	-
ka	-	r	ki	ya	-	-	-	bhi	gi	bhi	gi	ra	-	te	-
P	P	P	P	D	-	P	-	P	P	P	D	P	P	M	G
mi	thi	mi	thi	ba	-	te	-	au	r	main	ne	di	l	ko	ni
M	-	M	M	M	-	M	-	-	-	M	-	G	-	S	-
sa	-	r	ki	ya	-	ha	-	-	-	main	-	ne	-	bhi	-
R	-	R	R	R	-	-	-								
pya	-	r	ki	ya	-	-	-								

interlude:

flute: D--- NS'R'- D—S'N ND DP

synthe: RR MR RR PR RR PR RD RP DD S'D DR'S'N D-

piyano: R' S' D P, M G R S .D

1	2	3	4	5	6	7	8	1	2	3	4	5	6	7	8
D	-	D	D	D	-	D	N	R'	-	D	D	D	D	P	M
pya	-	r	ki	ya	-	k	li	yon	-	ke	m	h	k	te	-
P	-	P	-	P	-	-	-	P	-	P	P	P	-	D	N
an	-	go	-	se	-	-	-	pya	-	r	ki	ya	-	main	ne

S' -   D   D | P   -   M   G | M   -   M   - | M   -   -   -
gul -   ke gu| la -   bi - | ga -   lo - | se -   -   -

M R' S' M R' S' D S' N P N D D D R'
ha ha ha ha ha ha aa aa aa aa aa aa aa aa aa

D   -   D   D | D   -   D   N | R' -   D   D | D   -   P   M
pya -   r   ki| ya -   n   r | gi -s ki n | shi -   li -

P   -   P   - | P   -   -   - | P   -   P   P | P   -   D   N
aan -   khon - | se -   -   - | pya -   r   ki| ya -   b   d

S' -   D   D | P   -   M   G | M   -   M   - | M   -   -   -
li -   ki rn| gi -   li - | zu l   fo - | se -   -   -

S' S' -   S'| -   S' S' - | R' D   D   R'| D   -   -   -
khu li -   chan| - d   ni - | me -   ha ha| ha -   -   -

S' S' -   S'| -   S' S' - | R' -   D   - | D   -   P   M
khu li -   chan| - d   ni - | me -   main - | ne -   a   bhi

P   -   P   P | P   -   M   - | -   -   M   - | G   -   S   -
sa -   r   ki| ya -   ha - | -   -   main - | ne -   bhi -

R   -   R   R | R   -   -
pya -   r   ki| ya -   -

interlude: as above.

D   -   D   D | D   -   D   N | R' -   D   D | D   D   P   M
tha -   m   li| ya -   sii - | ne -   pe u | chh l   ti -

P   P   P   - | P   -   -   - | P   -   P   P | P   -   D   N
l   h   ro - | ko -   -   - | jhu -   m   u | tha -   ba -

S' -   D   D | P   P   M   G | M   -   M   - | M   -   -   -
ho -   me p | k   d   tu - | fa -   no - | ko -   -   -

M R' S' M R'S'   D S' <u>N</u> P <u>N</u> D   D D R'
ha ha ha ha ha ha aa aa aa aa aa aa aa aa aa

D	-	D	D	D	-	D	<u>N</u>	R'	-	D	D	D	D	P	M
chu	-	m	li	ya	-	bi	j	li	-	se	m	ch	I	te	-
P	-	P	-	P	-	-	-	P	-	P	P	P	-	D	<u>N</u>
ho	-	tho	-	ko	-	-	-	lu	-	t	li	ya	-	main	ne
S'	-	D	D	P	P	M	G	M	-	M	-	M	-	-	-
m	s	t	u	bh	r	ti	b	ha	-	ro	-	ko	-	-	-
S'	-	S'	S'	S'	S'	S'	S'	R'	D	D	R'	D	-	-	-
ra	-	t	ki	du	I	h	n	ka	-	aa	ha	ha	-	-	-
S'	-	S'	S'	S'	S'	S'	S'	R'	-	D	-	D	-	P	M
ra	-	t	ki	du	I	h	n	ka	-	main	-	ne	-	sin	-
P	-	P	P	P	-	M	-	-	-	M	-	G	-	S	-
ga	-	r	ki	ya	-	ha	-	-	-	main	-	ne	-	bhi	-
R	-	R	R	R	-	-									
pya	-	r	ki	ya	-	-									

24. HAAL E DIL UNKO SUNANA THA

Film: Fariyad (1964)   Music: Snehal Bhaatkar
Lyrics: Kedar Sharma   Singer: Suman K.
Taal: Daadra   Chord: RMD   S=C#

haal-e-dil unako sunaana tha -2
sunaaya na gaya, sunaaya na gaya
jo zubaan par mujhe laana tha
wo laaya na gaya, wo laaya na gaya

pyaar se sine pe sar rakhake to dil kadamon pe -2
apako apana banaana tha -2
banaaya na gaya, banaaya na gaya

khelati ankh-michauli rahi nazaren apani -2
jinako palakon men chhupaana tha -2
chhupaaya na gaya, chhupaaya na gaya

ek hi waar men haathon se jigar thaam liya -2
haay jis dil ko bachaana tha -2
bachaaya na gaya, bachaaya na gaya

HAAL E DIL UNKO SUNANA THA

dha	dhi	na	dha	tun	na	dha	dhi	na	dha	tun	na
1	2	3	4	5	6	1	2	3	4	5	6
prelude: S' M'- S' R'- S' M'- R' P'— S' R'-											
R'S'DPMR-　RMPDR'-　S'ND-											
								R'	R'	S'	D
								ha	le	dil	-
S'	R'	-	D	M	-	P	-	D	-	S'	-
un	ko	-	su	na	-	na	-	tha	-	-	-
R'	-	R'	R'	S'	D	S'	R'	-	D	M	-
-	-	ha	le	dil	-	un	ko	-	su	na	-
P	-	D	-	-	-	-	-	-	S'	P	D
na	-	tha	-	-	-	-	-	-	su	na	-
R'	-	-	-	D	P	D	-	-	S'	P	G'
ya	-	-	-	na	g	ya	-	-	su	na	-
G'	-	R'	-	D	P	D	-	-	PD	S'D	P
ya	-	-	-	na	g	ya	-	-	-	-	-
M	-	D	D	P	M	P	-	M	G	GM	P
-	-	jo	zu	ba	-	pr	-	mu	jhe	la-	-
G	-	R	-	-	-				S'	P	D
na	-	tha	-	-	-				vo	la	-
R'	-	-	-	D	P	D	-	-	S'	P	G'
ya	-	-	-	na	g	ya	-	-	vo	la	-
G'	-	R'	-	D	P	D	-	R'	R'	S'	D
ya	-	-	-	na	g	ya	-	ha	le	dil	-

S'	R'	-									
un	ko	-									

prelude: S' M'- S' R'- S' M'- R' P'— S' R'-
R'S'DPMR- RMPDR'- S'ND-

								S'	S'	S'	-
								pya	r	se	-

NS'	R'	N	D	D	-	P	-	D	P	M	-
sii-	-	ne	pe	sr	-	r	kh	ke	to	dil	-

M	P	D	S'	N	-	D	-	D	-D	P	M
q	d	mo	-	pr	-	-	-	aa	-p	ko	-

M	P	M	G	GM	P	G	-	R	-	-	-
a	p	na	b	na-	-	na	-	tha	-	-	-

-	-	-	S'	P	D	R'	-	-	-	S'	P
-	-	-	b	na	-	ya	-	-	-	na	g

D	-	-	S'	P	G'	G'	-	R'	-	S'	P
ya	-	-	b	na	-	ya	-	-	-	na	g

D	-	R'	R'	S'	D	S'	R'	-
ya	-	ha	le	dil	-	un	ko	-

prelude: S' M'- S' R'- S' M'- R' P'— S' R'-
R'S'DPMR- RMPDR'- S'ND-

PDR'   R'R'R'   R'R'S'   DN PMMP DS'ND
khelti aankh-michauli rhi nzren- apni –

D D   PM P M G GMP   G R
jinko plko me chhupa-- na tha

S'PDR'   S' PD R' PG'G'R'   S' PD
chhupa-ya na gya, chhupa-ya- na gya

R'R'   S'D   S' R'
hale   dil- unko

DS' PD R'R' R' R'S'S'R'G' R' S'S' NS' R' S' R' N D
ek hi- var me ha-tho---   se jigr tham liya------

 D   PM   P M GGMP   G R
hay jis   dil ko bchha-- na tha

S'PDR'   S' PD   R' PG'G'R'   S' PD
bchha-ya   na gya, bchha-ya-   na gya

R'R'   S'D   S' R'
hale   dil- unko

25. HAI NA BOLO BOLO

Film: Andaz (1971)   Music: Shanker Jaikishan
Lyrics: Hasrat Jaipuri   Singer: Suman K., Md. Rafi, Sushma
Taal: Kaharwa   Shreshtha, Pratibha
Chord: GPN   S=D

hai na bolo bolo -2 paapa bolo bolo mammi bolo bolo
paapa ko mammi se, mammi ko paapa se, pyaar hai pyaar hai

paapa mammi milate hain, chupake chupake hansate hain -2
jaane kyaa kya kahate hain, baaten karate rahate hain
hai na bolo bolo....

mammi teri achchhi hai kitani bholi bhaali hai
paapa bhi to achchhe hain kitane pyaare pyaare hain
hai na bolo bolo-2 munni bolo bolo dipu bolo bolo
paapa ko mammi se mammi ko paapa se pyaar hai pyaar hai
hai na bolo bolo....

papa se main bolungi mammi ko ghar le aayein
mammi se main bolunga saath mujhe bhi le jaayein
mammi bolo bolo, papa bolo bolo,
paapa ko mammi se mammi ko paapa se pyaar hai pyaar hai
hai na bolo bolo -2
paapa ko dipu se mammi ko munni se pyaar hai pyaar hai.

HAI NA BOLO BOLO

dha	ge	n	ti	n	ke	dhi	n	dha	ge	n	ti	n	ke	dhi	n
1	2	3	4	5	6	7	8	1	2	3	4	5	6	7	8
prelude: S G S G S G S G															
G	-	G	-	-	G	G	G	G	-	-	-	M	-	M	-
hai	-	na	-	-	bo	lo	bo	lo	-	-	-	hai	-	na	-
-	M	M	M	M	-	-	-	G	-	G	-	-	G	G	G
-	bo	lo	bo	lo	-	-	-	pa	-	pa	-	-	bo	lo	bo
G	-	-	-	M	-	M	-	-	M	M	M	M	-	-	-
lo	-	-	-	m	-	mmi	-	-	bo	lo	bo	lo	-	-	-
P	P	P	-	P	P	P	-	D	D	D	-	D	D	D	-
pa	pa	ko	-	m	mmi	se	-	m	mmi	ko	-	pa	pa	se	-
N	-	-	-	D	-	-	-	N	-	-	-	D	-	-	-
pya	-	-	r	hai	-	-	-	pya	-	-	r	hai	-	-	-
interlude: N G' R' N N M' G' R'															
P' M*' P' M*' D' P' M' G' M' G' P' M' N' D' P' M' G'---															
D	D	N	N	D	D	D	-	D	D	N	N	D	D	D	-
pa	pa	m	mmi	mil	te	hain	-	chup	ke	chup	ke	hns	te	hain	-
G	G	M	P	M	M	M	-	N	D	P	M	G	G	G	-
ja	ne	kya	kya	kh	te	hain	-	ba	te	kr	te	rh	te	hain	-
D	D	N	N	D	D	D	-	D	D	N	N	D	D	D	-
m	mmi	te	ri	a	chchhi	hai	-	kit	ni	bho	li	bha	li	hai	-
G	G	M	P	M	M	M	-	N	D	P	M	G	G	G	-
pa	pa	bhi	to	a	chchhe	hain	-	kit	ne	pya	re	pya	re	hain	-
D	D	N	N	D	D	D	-	D	D	N	N	D	D	D	-
pa	pa	se	main	bo	lu	gi	-	m	mmi	ko	ghr	le	aa	yen	-

G	G	M	P	M	M	M	-	N	D	P	M	G	G	G	-
m	mmi	se	main	bo	lu	ga	-	sa	-th	mujhe	bhi	le	ja	yen	-

G	-	G	-	-	G	G	G	G	-	-	-	M	-	M	-
hai	-	na	-	-	bo	lo	bo	lo	-	-	-	hai	-	na	-

-	M	M	M	M	-	-	-	G	-	G	-	-	G	G	G
-	bo	lo	bo	lo	-	-	-	pa	-	pa	-	-	bo	lo	bo

G	-	-	-
lo	-	-	-

26. ITNA HAI TUMSE PYAR MUJHE

Film: Suraj (1966)
Lyrics: Hasrat Jaipuri
Taal: Daadra

Music: Shanker Jaikishan
Singer: Md. Rafi, Suman K.
Chord: SGP   S=D#

R: itna hai tumse pyaar mujhe mere raazdaar
       jitne ke aasmaan par taare hai beshumaar

S: itna hai tumse pyaar mujhe mere raazdaar
       jitne ke iss zameen par zarre hai beshumaar

B: itna hai tumse pyaar mujhe mere raazdaar

R: tere siwaa kissi ko na laaya nigaah mein
       laakhon haseen aaye jawaani ki raah mein
       sadiyon se kar raha tha tumhaara hi intezaar

B: itna hai tumse pyaar mujhe mere raazdaar
       jitne ke aasmaan par taare hai beshumaar
       itna hai tumse pyaar mujhe mere raazdaar

S: maine bhi tere waaste kitne janam liye
       tab dil ke raasto pe jale pyaar ke diye
       ek din zaroor paaugi itna tha aitbaar

B: itna hai tumse pyaar mujhe mere raazdaar
       jitne ke iss zameen par zarre hai beshumaar
       itna hai tumse pyaar mujhe mere raazdaar

M: Bekhud banaa diya mujhe tere salaam ne
       Jannat agar mile to na loon tere saamne
       Yeh pyaar woh nasha hai ke jisska nahin utaar
       Itna hai tumse pyaar mujhe mere raazdaar

B: Itna hai tumse pyaar mujhe mere raazdaar

R: Jitne ke aasmaan par taare hai beshumaar

S: Itna hai tumse pyaar mujhe mere raazdaar
       Jitne ke iss zameen par zarre hai beshumaar

B: Itna hai tumse pyaar mujhe mere raazdaar.

ITNA HAI TUMSE PYAR MUJHE

dha	dhi	na	dha	tu	na	dha	dhi	na	dha	tu	na
1	2	3	4	5	6	1	2	3	4	5	6
prelude: S'R'R'S', NS'S'N, DNND, PDDP, MPPM, GMMG, RGGR, S–											
										S i	S t
M	–	R	G	S	S	M	–	R	G	S	–
na	–	hai	tum	–	se	pya	–	r	mu	jhe	–
P	–	P	P	D	M*	P	–	-P	–	G	P
me	–	re	ra	–	z	da	–	-r	–	ji	t
DN	S'	S'	S'	–	S'	NS'	R'	S'	N	P	P
ne -	–	ke	aa	–	s	ma -	–	n	pr	–	ta
N	–	N	D	–	M*	DP	MG	PM	GR	–	SS
re	–	hain	be	–	shu	ma-	--	--	-r	–	it
M	–	R	G	S	S	M	–	R	G	S	–
na	–	hai	tum	–	se	pya	–	r	mu	jhe	–
P	–	P	P	D	M*	P	–	-P	–	G	P
me	–	re	ra-	–	z	da	–	-r	–	ji	t
DN	S'	S'	S'	S'	S'	NS'	R'	S'	N	P	P
ne -	–	ke	i	s	j	mi-	–	n	pr	–	z
N	–	N	D	–	M*	DP	MG	PM	GR	–	SS
rre	–	hain	be	–	shu	ma-	--	--	-r	–	it
M	–	R	G	S	S	M	–	R	G	S	–
na	–	hai	tum	–	se	pya	–	r	mu	jhe	–
P	–	P	P	D	M*	P	–	–			
me	–	re	ra	–	z	da	–	-r			

interlude:
S' GPS' S' GPS' S'G'R'G'S'R' NS'DNP
N GPN N GPN NR' S'R' NS' DN P-
santur: GP S'NP- GP NDP- GP DPMG P- P- x2

										N	D
										te	-
N	P	P	P	-	M*	D	P	P	P	P	-
re	-	si	va	-	ki	sii	-	ko	n	la	-
P	S	R	GM	P	M	G	R	G	-	N	D
ya	-	ni	ga -	-	h	me	-	-	-	la	-
N	P	P	P	-	M*	D	P	P	P	P	-
khon	-	h	sii	-	n	aa	-	ye	j	va	-
S	-	R	GM	P	M	GS	G	-	-	G	P
ni	-	ki	ra -	-	h	me -	-	-	-	s	di
DN	S'	S'	S'	S'	S'	NS'	R'	S'	N	P	D
yon-	-	se	k	r	r	ha -	-	tha	tu	mha	-
N	-	S'	D	-	M*	DP	MG	PM	GR	-	SS
ra	-	hi	in	-	t	za-	--	--	-r	-	it
M	-	R	G	S	S	M	-	R	G	S	-
na	-	hai	tum	-	se	pya	-	r	mu	jhe	-
P	-	P	P	D	M*	P	-	-			
me	-	re	ra	-	z	da	-	-r			

interlude:

PGP-N-, PGP-N-, PGP-N- D- P- x2

GMPDNS'R'G' P' P', DDDD N- S'S'S'S' S'-

GP M*P M*P, GP M*P M*P, GP M*P M*P N-

				N	D
				main	-

N	P	P	P	-	M*	D	P	P	P	P	P
ne	-	bhi	te	-	re	va	-	s	te	ki	t
P	S	R	GM	P	M	G	-	-	-	N	D
ne	-	j	nm	-	li	ye	-	-	-	t	b
N	P	P	P	-	M*	D	P	P	P	P	-
dil	-	ke	ra	-	s	to	-	pe	j	le	-
S	-	R	GM	P	M	G	-	-	-	G	P
pya	-	r	ke	-	di	ye	-	-	-	i	k
DN	S'	S'	S'	-	S'	NS'	R'	S'	N	P	GP
din	-	z	ru	-	r	pa	-	un	gi	-	it
N	-	N	D	-	M*	DP	MG	PM	GR	-	SS
na	-	tha	ae	-	t	ba-	--	--	-r	-	it
M	-	R	G	S	S	M	-	R	G	S	-
na	-	hai	tum	-	se	pya	-	r	mu	jhe	-
P	-	P	P	D	M*	P	-	-			
me	-	re	ra	-	z	da	-	-r			

interlude: S' GPS' S' GPS' S'G'R'G'S'R' NS'DNP
N GPN N GPN NR' S'R' NS' DN P-
santur: GP S'NP- GP NDP- GP DPMG P- P- x2

NDNP   PP   M*DP   PP   PS RGMPM   GSG
be-khud bna diya- mujhe tere sla--m   ne—

NDNP PP   M*DP   P P P S-R   GPMGSG
jnnt   agr mile-   to n lu te-re   sa-mne—

GP   DNS'S'   S'   S'S'R'   N   N   PD   N   ND M*DPMGPMGR
ye   pya--r   vo   nsha-   hai ke jiska nhin uta---------r

27. JUHI KI KALI MERI LADLI

Film: Dil Ek Mandir (1963)   Music: Shanker Jaikishan
Lyrics: Shailendra   Singer: Suman K.
Taal: Daadra   Chord: RMD S=C#

juhi ki kali meri laadali naazo ki pali meri laadali
o aas kiran jug jug tu jiye
nanhi si pari meri laadali o meri laadali

dharti pe utar aaya chanda tera chehra bana
champe kaa salaunaa guladastaa tan tera bana -2
o meri laadali
komal titali meri laadali hire ki kani meri laadali
o aas kiran jug jug tu jie
nanhi si pari meri laadali o meri laadali

sharmaae divaali taaro ki tere naino se
koyal ne churaai hai pacham tere baino se -2
o meri laadali
gudiyaa si dhali meri laadali mohe laage bhali meri laadali
o aas kiran jug jug tu jie
nanhi si pari meri laadali o meri laadali

har bol tera sikhalaae hame dukh se ladanaa
muskaan teri kahati hai sada dhiraj dharna -2
o meri laadali
gangaa ki lahar meri laadali chanchal saagar meri laadali
o aas kiran jug jug tu jie
nanhi si pari meri laadali o meri laadali
juhi ki kali meri laadali......

JUHI KI KALI MERI LADLI

dhin	-	ti	na	dhin	na	dhin	-	ti	na	dhin	na
1	2	3	4	5	6	1	2	4	5	6	8
prelude: M- P- M R S R M -											D
											ju
D	D	P	P	M	G	R	-	R	R	-	D
hi	ki	k	li	me	ri	la	-	d	li	-	na
D	D	P	P	M	G	R	-	R	R	-	N
jo	se	p	li	me	ri	la	-	d	li	-	o
N	-	N	N	N	D	D	S'	N	N	-	R'
aa	-s	ki	rn	ju	g	jug	tu	ji	ye	-	nn
R'	R'	S'	N	D	P	M	-	M	M	-	G
hin	sii	p	ri	me	ri	la	-	d	li	-	-
M	-	R	G	M	-	R	-	R	R	-	-
-	-	o	me	ri	-	la	-	d	li	-	-

interlude:
S' D N S' M' R' S' D –
S' D N S' G' S' N P –
PDN --- M MPD--- G GMP--- G – R –

dhin	-	ti	na	dhin	na	dhin	-	ti	na	dhin	na
1	2	3	4	5	6	1	2	4	5	6	8
										R'	R'
										dh	r
R'	R'	R'	S'	S'	-	N	N	-	D	M	P
ti	pe	u	tr	aa	-	ya	chn	-	da	te	ra
D	D	D	D	-	-	-	-	-	-	R'	-
cheh	ra	b	na	-	-	-	-	-	-	chn	-

R'	R'	R'	S'	S'	-	N	N	-	D	M	P
pe	ka	s	lau	na	-	gul	d	-	sta	t	n
D	D	D	D	-	-	-	-	-	-	M'	-
te	ra	b	na	-	-	-	-	-	-	chn	-
M'	R'	S'	N	M	-	P	M	-	M	N	D
pe	ka	s	lau	na	-	gul	d	-	sta	t	n
P	M	M	M	-	G	M	-	R	G	M	-
te	ra	b	na	-	-	-	-	o	me	ri	-
R	-	R	R	-	-	-	-	-	-	-	D
la	-	d	li	-	-	-	-	-	-	-	ko
D	D	P	P	M	G	R	-	R	R	-	D
ml	ti	t	li	me	ri	la	-	d	li	-	hi
D	D	P	P	M	G	R	-	R	R	-	N
re	ki	k	ni	me	ri	la	-	d	li	-	o
N	-	N	N	N	D	D	S'	N	N	-	R'
aa	-s	ki	rn	ju	g	jug	tu	ji	ye	-	nn
R'	R'	S'	N	D	P	M	-	M	M	-	G
hin	sii	p	ri	me	ri	la	-	d	li	-	-
M	-	R	G	M	-	R	-	R	R	-	-
-	-	o	me	ri	-	la	-	d	li	-	-

28. KABHI HOTON SE MUJHE BHI LAGA

Film: Geet (1970)
Lyrics: Prem Dhawan
Taal: Kaharwa dugun

Music: Kalyanji Anandji
Singer: Suman K.
Chord: GPN   S=C#

kya hai iss bansuriya mein
jo mujhme nahi sanvariya
kabhi hontho se mujhe bhi laga le
bansuri banai ke ho bansuri banai ke

mai toh gaaun, mai toh gaaun tere giit mere miit
sare jag ko bhulai ke
kabhi hontho se mujhe bhi laga le
bansuri banai ke ho bansuri banai ke -2

tore sang neha laga tore rang rachi -2
ban ban dware dware phiru madmati
tujhmein hi, tujhmein hi sama gayi
main tere pas aayi ke
kabhi hontho se mujhe bhi laga le
bansuri banai ke ho bansuri banai ke -2

sara jag jan gaya radha bhai shyam ki -2
chhede teraa nam leke sakhiyan sare ganv ki
ho chhaliya tune
chhaliya tune sudh naa lini baanvari banai ke
kabhi hontho se mujhe bhi laga le
bansuri banai ke ho bansuri banai ke -2

KABHI HOTON SE MUJHE BHI LAGA

dhage	nti	nke	dhin	dhage	nti	nke	dhin	dhage	nti	nke	dhin	dhage	nti	nke	dhin
12	34	56	78	12	34	56	78	12	34	56	78	12	34	56	78

prelude:
P M*G M*P , D PM* PD
N S' N D -4
R' R' R' N -4
R' G' R' R' -4
M*' P' M*' G' -4
R' N P M* G
flute: G' --- G' M*' G' P' M*' G' R' S' N
     N---- R' S' N N , R' S' N, N P-- R G

N	N	NN	NR'R'N	N	N	N	NNS'D	PM*PG	GM*DP--		M* G

kya hai.... is ba- suri ya me, jo mujhme...nhin.... S'vriya

										G	G
										k	bhi

G	P	D	N	D	-S'	N	M*	P	-	- M*	P	-	G	-
ho	to	se	mu	jhe bhi	-		l	ga	-	- -	le	-	-	-

-	G	PD	-N	D	-P	-	M*	D	P	M*	G	G	-	M*	G
-	ba	suri	-b	naii -ke	-		ho	ba	su	ri	b	na	ii	ke	-

-	G	PD	-N	D	-P	-	M*	D	P	M*	G	G	G	D	D
-	ba	suri	-b	naii -ke	-		ho	ba	su	ri	b	naii	ke	main	to

N	-	D	D	-	-	-	-	-	-	-	-	-	-	D	D
ga	-	un	-	-	-	-	-	-	-	-	-	-	-	main	to

N	N	D	D	N	-	D	D	N	-	N	D	N	R'R'	-	N
ga	un	te	re	gi	-t	me	re	mi	-t	sa	re	j	gko	-	bhu

D	-	P^D	-	M*^P	-	G	G	G	P	D	N	D	-S'	N	M*
la	ii	ke	-	-	-	k	bhi	ho	to	se	mu	jhe bhi	-		l

P	-	-	M*	P	-	G	-	-	G	PD	-N	D	-P	-	M*
ga	-	-	-	le	-	-	-	-	ba	suri	-b	naii	-ke	-	ho

D	P	M*	G	G	-	M*	G	-	G	PD	-N	D	-P	-	M*
ba	su	ri	b	na	ii	ke	-	-	ba	suri	-b	naii	-ke	-	ho

D	P	M*	G	G	G	G	-
ba	su	ri	b	na	ii	ke	-

interlude:

GPP M*DD PN

DR'R' NR'R' R'G'

G' P' M*' G' R' R' N D

N R' R' N D P M* G

flute:

G M* G – G N- N-

N R' R' N N- R'ND

D D D D D D D

N D P M* G – D-

D D D D D D D, N D P M* G -

N	-	-	-	-	-	R'	R'	G'	R'	N	P	N	-	-	-
ho	-	-	-	-	-	-	-	-	-	-	-	-	-	-	-

-	N	S'D	-D	P	M*	D	D	-	N	R'R'-G'		R'	-	R'	
-	to	resn	-g	ne	ha	la	ga	-	to	rern	-g	ra	-	chi	-

-	R'	R'N	-D	P	M*	D	D	-	N	R'R'-G'		R'	-	R'	
-	to	resn	-g	ne	ha	la	ga	-	to	rern	-g	ra	-	chi	-

-	R'	R'N	-D	P	M*	D	D	-	N	R'R'-G'		R'	-	R'	
-	b	nb	-n	dwa	re	dwa	re	-	fi	rum	-d	ma	-	ti	-

D	R'R'	R'	G'G'	R'	-	R'	N	D	DD	-	D	-	-	-	-
-	-	-	-	-	-	o	-	tu	jhme	-	hi	-	-	-	-

DD	D	D	D	D	-D	D	D	N	R'	R'	-N	D	-	P	-
tujh	me	hi	s	ma	-g	yi	main	te	re	pa	-s	aa	ii	ke	-

M*	-	G	G	G	P	D	N	D	-S'	N	M*	P	-	-	M*
-	-	k	bhi	ho	to	se	mu	jhe	-bhi	-	I	ga	-	-	-

P	-	G	-	-	G	PD	-N	D	-P	-	M*	D	P	M*	G
le	-	-	-	-	ba	suri	-b	naii	-ke	-	ho	ba	su	ri	b

G	-	M*	G	-	G	PD	-N	D	-P	-	M*	D	P	M*	G
na	ii	ke	-	-	ba	suri	-b	naii	-ke	-	ho	ba	su	ri	b

G	G	G	-
na	ii	ke	-

interlude:

G PP M* DD PN

D S'S' D R'R' S'G'

G'P'M*'G'R'R'ND NR'R'NDPM*G

flute:

G M* G – G N- N-

N R' R' N N- R'ND

D D D D D D D

N D P M* G – D-

D D D D D D D

N D P M* G –

NNNN NR'R'G' G'R'NP N---

o...

NS' DD PM* DD NR' R'G' R'R'   R'

sara jg   jan gya radha bhyi shyam ki

R'R' ND PM* DD NR'   R'G' R'R'   R'

sara jg   jan   gya radha bhyi shyam ki

R'R'   ND PM* DD N R' R'G' R'R'   R'

chhede tera   nam leke sakhiya sare ganv ki

```
R'ND  DD   DD
ho     chhliya tune


DD      DD     D  D  DD   NR'R'  ND  P- M*-
chhliya  tune sudh  na linhi bavri   bnaii ke


GG  GP  D ND    S'N   M*P-M*  P G
kbhi hoto se mujhe   bhi- lga--     le


GPD   ND  P  M*  DPM*  GG  M*G
basuri bnaii ke ho basuri bnaii  ke


GPD   ND   P  M*  DPM*  GG  G
basuri bnaii ke ho basuri bnaii ke
```

29. KE JAAN CHALI JAYE JIYA NAHIN JAAY

Film: Anjana (1969)   Music: Laxmikant Pyarelal
Lyrics: Anand Bakshi   Singer: Md. Rafi, Suman K.
Taal: Kaharwa   Chord: SGP RP$\underline{N}$ S=C

qaraar khoyaa mohabbat mein is zamaane ne
yeh baat sach hi kahi hai kisi deewaane ne

ke jaan chali jaaye jiyaa nahin jaaye
jiyaa jaaye to phir jiyaa nahin jaaye
yeh ilzaam sar pe liyaa nahin jaaye
liyaa jaaye to phir jiyaa nahin jaaye
ke jaan chali jaaye ho ooooo

zamaane mein nahin deewaana ham saa -2
deewaana nahin yeh zamaana ham saa
yeh kya jaane, yeh kya samjhe, yeh baatein pyaar ki -2
ooo.. ke pyaar har kisi se kiyaa nahin jaaye
kiyaa jaaye to phir jiyaa nahin jaaye
ke jaan chali jaaye ho ooo

na aaye kabhi neend, na aaya hai qaraar -2

hamaari taubaa ham nahin karenge pyaar

bas laao dil hamaara ham ko de do o sanam-2

o o... yeh dil le ke waapas diyaa nahin jaaye

diyaa jaaye to phir jiyaa nahin jaaye

ke jaan chali jaaye ho ooo

churaa ke nazren na dekho tum yeh phool -2

suno yeh be-rukhi hamen nahin qubool

yaa ham jaayen yaa keh do yeh bahaar chali jaaye -2

o o... bahaar chali jaaye piyaa nahin jaaye

piyaa jaaye to phir jiyaa nahin jaaye

ke jaan chali jaaye jiyaa nahin jaaye

jiyaa jaaye to phir jiyaa nahin jaaye

ke jaan chali jaaye ho........

KE JAAN CHALI JAYE JIYA NAHIN JAAY

dhin	-	-	ta	-	-	ta	-	dhindhin	-	ta	-	-	ta	-
1	2	3	4	5	6	7	8	1	2	3	4	5	6	7	8

prelude:

S'S'S' R'R'   R'R'G'R'G' S' NN   NNR'D   P
qrar   khoya mohbbt me is   zmane   ne

P   PP   DP M   SRP P   PP   PDPD P   M
yh bat sch hi khi- hai kisii diva--ne ne

												S'	-
												ke	-
N	S'	-	-	-	D	P	-	P	D	-	P	M	-	M	-
ja	-	-	-	n	ch	li	-	ja	-	-	ye	-	-	ji	-

| R | M | - | - | - | P | D̲ | - | N̲ | - | - | - | - | - | - | - |
| ya | - | - | - | - | n | hin | - | ja | - | - | - | - | y | - | - |

| - | - | G' | R' | - | G' | - | M' | G' | - | - | S' | - | - | S' | - |
| - | - | ji | ya | - | ja | - | ye | to | - | - | fi | - | r | ji | - |

| N | - | - | R' | - | S' | D̲ | - | D̲ | - | - | - | - | S' | S' | - |
| ya | - | - | - | - | n | hin | - | ja | - | - | - | - | y | ye | - |

| N | S' | - | D̲ | - | - | P | - | P | D̲ | - | P | M | - | M | - |
| il | - | - | ja | - | - | m | - | sr | - | - | pe | - | - | li | - |

| R | M | - | - | - | P | D̲ | - | N̲ | - | - | - | - | - | - | - |
| ya | - | - | - | - | n | hin | - | ja | - | - | - | - | y | - | - |

| - | - | G' | R' | - | G' | - | M' | G' | - | - | S' | - | - | S' | - |
| - | - | li | ya | - | ja | - | ye | to | - | - | fi | - | r | ji | - |

| N | - | - | R' | - | S' | D̲ | - | D̲ | - | - | - | - | S' | S' | - |
| ya | - | - | - | - | n | hin | - | ja | - | - | - | - | y | ke | - |

| N | S' | - | - | - | D̲ | P | - | P | D̲ | - | P | M | - | - | - |
| ja | - | - | - | n | ch | li | - | ja | - | - | ye | - | - | - | - |

| - | - | R | - | N̲ | - | D̲ | - | P | - | - | - | - | - | - | - |
| - | - | ho | - | o | - | o | - | o | - | - | - | - | - | - | - |

interlude:

P P D̲ N̲ R' S' N̲ D̲ – 2 G' R' S' N̲ D̲ P

M P P M M D̲ D̲ P P N̲ N̲ D̲ D̲ P P P – 2 G' R' S' N̲ D̲ P

M P P M P D̲ D̲ P P N̲ N̲ D̲ D̲ P P P -2

G' R' G' R' G' R' P'----   G' R' G' R' G' R' S'----

														S'	-
														z	-
S'	-	R'	-	S'	-	R'	-	G'	-	-	-	-	-	G'	-
ma	-	ne	-	me	-	n	-	hin	-	-	-	-	-	di	-

R'	-	G'	-	-	-	R'	S'	S'	-	-	-	-	-	S'	-
va	-	na	-	-	-	h	m	sa	-	-	-	-	-	di	-
S'	-	R'	-	D	S'	R'	-	G'	-	-	-	-	-	G'	-
va	-	na	-	-	n	hin	-	ye	-	-	-	-	-	z	-
R'	-	G'	-	-	-	R'	S'	S'	-	-	-	-	-	G'	-
ma	-	na	-	-	-	h	m	sa	-	-	-	-	-	ye	-
S'	-	G'	-	S'	-	R'	-	N	-	S'	-	D	-	N	-
kya	-	ja	-	ne	-	ye	-	kya	-	sm	-	jhe	-	ye	-
M	-	M	-	D	-	-	P	P	-	-	-	-	-	-	-
ba	-	te	-	pya	-	-	r	ki	-	-	-	-	-	-	-
S'	-	-	-	-	-	-	-	-	-	-	-	-	-	S'	-
o	-	-	-	-	-	-	-	-	-	-	-	-	-	ke	-
N	-	S'	-	D	D	-	D	P	D	-	P	M	-	M	-
pya	-	-	-	r	h	r	ki	sii	-	-	se	-	-	ki	-
R	M	-	-	-	P	D	-	N	-	-	-	-	-	-	-
ya	-	-	-	-	n	hin	-	ja	-	-	-	-	y		
-	-	G'	R'	-	G'	-	M'	G'	-	-	S'	-	-	S'	-
-	-	ki	ya	-	ja	-	ye	to	-	-	fi	-	r	ji	-
N	-	-	R'	-	S'	D	-	D	-	-	-	-	S'		
ya	-	-	-	-	n	hin	-	ja	-	-	-	-	y		

interlude:

P PP P DPMP P S' S' S'S'

S'R'R'S' NS'S'N DNND DNNP

P PP P DPMP P S' S' S'S'

S'R'R'S' NS'S'N P----

P P M P DS' D— S' D S' P ----
P P M P DS' D— S' D S' P ----
P'M' P'- D'- P'M'G'R' G'- M'- G'R'S'N   S'- R'- S'NDN P—

														S'	-
														na	-
S'	-	R'	-	S'	-	R'	-	G'	-	-	-	-	-	G'	-
aa	-	ye	-	k	-	bhi	-	nin	-	-	-	-	d	na	-
R'	-	G'	-	-	R'	-	S'	S'	-	-	-	-	-	S'	-
aa	-	ya	-	-	hai	-	q	ra	-	-	-	-	r	h	-
S'	-	R'	-	S'	-	R'	-	G'	-	-	-	-	-	G'	-
ma	-	ri	-	tau	-	ba	-	hm	-	-	-	-	-	n	-
R'	-	G'	-	R'	-	S'	-	S'	-	-	-	-	-	G'	-
hin	-	k	-	ren	-	ge	-	pya	-	-	-	-	r	b	s
S'	-	G'	-	S'	-	R'	-	N	-	S'	-	D	-	N	-
la	-	o	-	di	l	h	-	ma	-	ra	-	h	m	ko	-
M	-	M	-	D	-	P	-	P	-	-	-	-	-	-	-
de	-	do	-	o	-	s	-	nm	-	-	-	-	-	-	-
S'	-	-	-	-	-	-	-	-	-	-	-	-	-	S'	-
o	-	-	-	-	-	-	-	-	-	-	-	-	-	ye	-
N	-	S'	-	D	-	D	-	P	D	-	P	-	M	M	-
dil	-	-	-	le	-	ke	-	va	-	-	p	-	s	di	-
R	M	-	-	-	P	D	-	N	-	-	-	-	-	-	-
ya	-	-	-	-	n	hin	-	ja	-	-	-	-	y	-	-
-	-	G'	R'	-	G'	M'	-	G'	-	-	S'	-	-	S'	-
-	-	di	ya	-	ja	y	-	to	-	-	fi	-	r	ji	-

| N | - | - | R' | - | S' | D | - | D | - | - | - | - | S' |

| ya | - | - | - | - | n | hin | - | ja | - | - | - | - | y |

interlude:

P S' S' --- M- P- PD- D

PMPM DPDP S'N R'S' ND DP

PMPM DPDP S'N ND DP

R'S'--- G'R'--- M'G'----

S'S'   R' S'R'G' G' R'G' R' S' S'
chura ke nzren n dekho tum yh ful -2

S'S'   R' S' R' G' G'R' G'R' S'S'
suno yh be-rukhi hme nhin qubul

G' S' G'S' R' N S' D NMD DP P
ya hm jaen ya kh do ye bahar chli jae -2

S'--------

o -------

S'NS' DP PDPM MRM PD N
bahar chli ja-e- piya- nhin jae

G'R' G'M' G' S' S'NR' S'D DS'
piya jae to fir jiya- nhin jae

S' NS' DP PDPM MRM PD N
ke jan chli ja-e- jiya- nhin jae

G'R' G'M' G' S' S'NR' S'D DS'
jiya jae to fir jiya- nhin jae

S' NS' DP PDPM R N D P -
ke jan chli ja-e- o-------

30. KAUNE RANG MUNGWA

Film: Heera Moti (1959)   Music: Raushan Nagrath
Lyrics: Prem Dhawan   Singer: Suman K., Sudha Malhotra
Taal: Kaharwa dugun   Chord: M<u>D</u>S'   S=C

kaune rang mungwa kawan rang motiyaa kaune rang mungwa

kaune rang mungwa kawan rang motiyaa

ho kaune rang ho kaune rang

nanadi tore birna ho o o o jee

sabaz rang mungwa safed rang motiyaa sabaz rang mungwa

sabaz rang mungwa safed rang motiyaa

saanwar rang ho saanwar rang bhave ri more birna

ho o o o jee

toot gayile mungwa bikhar gaile motiyaa toot gayile mungwa

toot gayile mungwa bikhar gaile motiyaa

bisar gaile haay bisar gaile bhave ri more birna

ho o o o jee

been laibo mungwa bator laibo motiyaa been laibo mungwa

been laibo mungwa bator laibo motiyaa

manaaye laibo, manaaye laibo nanadi tore birna

ho o o o jee

kit sohe mungwa kit sohe motiyaa kit sohe mungwa

kit sohe mungwa kit sohe motiyaa

ho kit sohe, ho kit sohe nanadi tore birna

ho o o o jee

mundri sohe mungwa bakiya sohe motiyaa mundri sohe mungwa

mundri sohe mungwa bakiya sohe motiyaa

titiriya sohe, ho titiriya sohe bhave ri more birna

ho o o o jee

ho ho ho ho ho ho ho ho ho ho ho ho ho ho ho ho

KAUNE RANG MUNGWA

dhage	nti	nkedhin	dhage	nti	nkedhin	dhage	nti	nkedhin	dhage	nti	nkedhin
12	34	56 78	12	34	56 78	12	34	56 78	12	34	56 78

prelude:

M – D̲ P M – G̲ R MM D̲ P M – G̲ R

M – D̲ P M – G̲ R MM D̲ P M M M -

M M M M	N̲ N̲ N̲ N̲	N̲ S' N̲ N̲	D P D -
kau ne rn g	mun g va k	v n rn g	mo ti ya -
M M M M	N̲ N̲ N̲ -	M -MMR D̲P	M PM - -
kau ne rn g	mun g va -	- flute	- - - -
M M M M	N̲ N̲ N̲ N̲	N̲ S' N̲ N̲	D P D D
kau ne rn g	mun g va k	v n rn g	mo ti ya ho
P D̲ P M	PP -D̲ P D̲	P D̲ M P	D̲ - P -
kau ne rn g	flute: ho	kau ne rn g	n - n -
M - P P	M M M -	D̲ - P -	D̲ - P -
di - to re	bi r na -	ho - o -	o - o -
M - - PD̲	M -P M M	M M M M	N̲ N̲ N̲ N̲
ji - - -	- - - s	b j rn g	mun g va s
N̲ S' N̲ N̲	D P D M	M M M M	N̲ N̲ N̲ -
fe d rn g	mo ti ya s	b j rn g	mun g va -

play rest of the song as above.
taan at the end
S'--------- R'G'R'G'S'---
ho--------------------

D – MP D- DD PP MM   MP DD PP MM
ho------------------   ho-----------

PDPDM- PDPDM-
ho------- ho-------

31. MAN MOHAN MAN MEIN HO TUMHI

Film: Kaise Kahun (1964)
Lyrics: Shakeel Badayuni
Taal: Teen Taal

Music: Sachindev Burman
Singer: Md. Rafi,Suman K., Shiv Dayal Batish
Chord: MD̲S' PN̲R'   S=C#

aa tanu um aa aa aa aa

aa aa aa aa aa aa

manmohan man me ho tumhi -2

more ang ang tumhi samaye

jano, ya jano na, ho tumhi

manmohan man me

manmohan man me, man me

ho tumhi, ho tumhi, ho tumhi

manmohan man me ho tumhi

more ang ang tumhi samaye

jano, ya jano na, ho tumhi

manmohan man me

dekh dekh tori chhab sanwariya -2

bani hain radha tumri banwariya

rom rom tumhare gun gaaye

mano, ya mano na, ho tumhi

manmohan man me

dekh dekh tori chhab sanwariya

hu bani hain radha tumhari banwariya

dekh dekh tori chhab sanwariya

bani hain radha tumri banwariya

rom rom tumhare gun gaaye

mano, ya mano na, ho tumhi

manmohan man me, manmohan man me

Vinod Kumar

MAN MOHAN MAN MEIN HO TUMHI

dha	dhin	dhin	dha	dha	dhin	dhin	dha	dha	tin	tin	ta	ta	dhin	dhin	dha
1	2	3	4	5	6	7	8	9	10	11	12	13	14	15	16

prelude:

```
S'-------S'NDNMP----        P MPN  G M
aa-------tanum--- --------  aa----------


M- S R --- S ---    M ----------
aa-------------- aa----------


M---- P----- MPN  D N P – GMP--- G ---
aa---------- aa------------------------


M—S--- R --- S   N P P M—P --
aa----------- aa---------
```

1	2	3	4	5	6	7	8	9	10	11	12	13	14	15	16
														M	P
														m	n
S'	-	S'	S'	N	R'	S'	-	-	D	-	N	P	-	P	P
mo	-	h	n	m	n	me	-	-	ho	-	tu	mhi	-	mo	re
M	P	P	M	G	G	G	G	M	-	-	S	R	-	S	-
an	-	g	an	-	g	tu	m	hi	-	-	s	ma	-	ye	-
S	S	S'	R'	-	N	S'	-	-	D	-	D	N	P	M	P
ja	no	ya	ja	-	no	na	-	-	ho	-	tu	mhi	-	m	n
S'	-	S'	S'	N	R'	S'	-	-	-	D	N	S'	-	-	-
mo	-	h	n	m	n	me	-	-	-	-	-	-	-	-	-
M	P	D	-	N	S'	-	R'	N	S'	-	R'	S'	R'	S'	R'
m	n	mo	-	h	n	-	m	n	me	-	m	-	n	-	me
M'	G'	M'	R'	S'	N	D	N	P	M	G	M	R	-	M	P
ho	-	-	tu	mhi	ho	-	tu	mhi	ho	-	tu	mhi	-	m	n

S'	-	S'	S'	N	R'	S'	-	-	D	-	N	P	-	P	P
mo	-	h	n	m	n	me	-	-	ho	-	tu	mhi	-	mo	re
M	P	P	M	G	G	G	G	M	-	-	S	R	-	S	-
an	-	g	an	-	g	tu	m	hi	-	-	s	ma	-	ye	-
S	S	S'	R'-	-	N	S'	-	-	D	-	D	N	P	M	P
ja	no	ya	ja	-	no	na	-	-	ho	-	tu	mhi	-	m	n
S'	-	S'	S'	N	R'	S'	-	-	-	D	N	S'	-	-	-
mo	-	h	n	m	n	me	-	-	-	-	-	-	-	-	-
M	-	P	N	-	D	N	N	S'	S'	S'	-	R'	N	S'	-
de	-	kh	de	-	kh	to	ri	chh	b	san	-	v	ri	ya	-
N	S'R'	-	R'	R'	-	M'	G'	G'	G'	G'	M'	R'	R'	S'	-
b	ni	-	hai	ra	-	dha	-	tu	mh	ri	ba	v	ri	ya	-
NS'	R'	R'	R'S'	S'	S'	N	P	M	G	G	M	R	-	S	-
ro-	-	m	ro-	-	m	tu	mh	re	-	gu	n	ga	-	ye	-
S	S	S'	R'	-	N	S'	N	S'	D	-	N	P	-	M	P
ma	no	ya	ma	-	no	na	-	-	ho	-	tu	mhi	-	m	n
S'	-	S'	S'	N	R'	S'	-	-	-	-	ND	N	-	P	-
mo	-	h	n	m	n	me	-	-	-	-	-	-	-	-	-
M	-	P	N	D	D	N	N	S'	S'	S'	-	R'	N	S'	-
de	-	kh	de	-	kh	to	ri	chh	b	san	-	v	ri	ya	-
-	-	-	-	D	N	-	P	-	N	S'	R'	R'	R'	-	R'
-	-	-	-	-	-	-	-	-	o	--	-	b	ni	-	hai
R'	-	G'	-	-	G'	R'S'	N	D	-	-	-	-	-	-	D
ra	-	dha	-	-	-	-	-	-	-	-	-	-	-	-	tu

D	M'	-	G'	-	-	-	-	S'	R'	-	-	R'	N	D	N
mh	-	-	ri	-	-	-	-	ba	v	-	-	ri	ya	-	-

M	-	P	N	D	D	N	N	S'	S'	S'	-	R'	N	S'	-
de	-	kh	de	-	kh	to	ri	chh	b	san	-	v	ri	ya	-

N	S'R'	-	R'	R'	-	M'	G'	G'	G'	G'	M'	R'	R'	S'	-
b	ni	-	hai	ra	-	dha	-	tu	mh	ri	ba	v	ri	ya	-

NS'	R'	R'	R'S'	S'	S'	N	P	M	G	G	M	R	-	S	-
ro-	-	m	ro-	-	m	tu	mh	re	-	gu	n	ga	-	ye	-

S	S	S'	R'	-	N	S'	N	S'	D	-	D	N	P	M	P
ma	no	ya	ma	-	no	na	-	-	ho	-	tu	mhi	-	m	n

S'	-	S'	S'	N	R'	S'	-	R'	-	S'	N	D	N	P	-
mo	-	h	n	m	n	me	-	-	-	-	-	-	-	-	-

R'------- $^{S'}$N--- D NS'R'---- $^{S'}$N--- D ---
aa------------------------------------

R'--- R'M'--- R'--- $^{S'}$N--- D --- R'--- $^{S'}$N--- D --- N R'---
aa--

M'---- R'---- M'R'S'ND---- N M'--- R'S'N R' S' S'R' R'M' M'P'---
aa--

32.   MERA PYAR BHI TU HAI

Film: Sathi (1968)
Lyrics: Majrooh Sultanpuri
Taal: Kaharwa

Music: Naushad Ali
Singer: Mukesh, Suman K.
Chord: RMD   S=C#

mera pyar bhi tu hai ye bahar bhi tu hai
tu hi nazro me jaan e tamanna
tu hi nazaro me nazaro me

tu hi to mera neel gagan hai
pyar se raoshan aankh uthae
aur ghata ke rup me tu hai
kandhe pe mere sar ko jhukaae
mujh pe late bhikhrae
mera pyar bhi tu hai...

manzil mere dil ki vahi hai
saya jaha dildar hai tera
parbat parbat teri bahein
gulshan gulshan pyar hai tera
mahke hai aanchal mera
mera pyar bhi tu hai...

jaagi nazar ka khvaab hai jaese
dekh milan ka din ye suhana
aankh to tere jalvo me gum hai
dekhu tujhe ya dekhu zamana
bekhud hai divana
mera pyar bhi tu hai....

MERA PYAR BHI TU HAI

dha	ge	n	ti	n	ke	dhi	n	dha	ge	n	ti	n	ke	dhi	n
1	2	3	4	5	6	7	8	1	2	3	4	5	6	7	8
prelude:															
N	-	-	-	-	-	-	-	G'	R'	S'	N	N	-	-	-
D	N	R'	G'	M'	-	-	-	-	-	-	-	-	G'	R'	N
R'	-	-	-	-	-									M	M
														me	ra
G	-	-	R	R	R	M	M	G	-	-	R	R	R	-	NN
pya	-	-r	bhi	tu	hai	ye	b	ha	-	-r	bhi	tu	hai	-	tuhi
DD	-N	-	D	P	-G	-	R	GP	M	G	-	-	R	R	R
nz	-ro	-	me	ja	-ne	-	t	mn-	-	na	-	-	tu	hi	n
GP	M*	G	R	R	-	-	R	GP	M*	G	R	R	-	-	-
za-	-	ro	-	me	-	-	n	za-	-	ro	-	me	-	-	-
G	-	-	D	M*	-	-	-	M	-	-	G	R	-	-	-
hu	-	-	-	-	-	-	-	-	-	-	-	-	-	-	-
interlude: D G' G' – G' G' G' N D ,															
M N – N N M D – M R --															
													D	D	D
													tu	-hi	-to
N	-	N	-	-	D	-D	-D	S'	N	N	-	-	D	-N	N
me	-	ra	-	-	ni	-l	-g	gn	-	hai	-	-	pya	-r	-se
R'	S'	S'	-	-	R'	- S'	-N	D	-	D	-	-	D	-N	R'N
rau	-	shn	-	-	aan	-kh	-u	tha	-	ye	-	-	au	-r	-gh
R'	-	R'	-	-	R'	-N	-D	N	-	D	-	N	-N	-	N
ta	-	ke	-	-	ru	-p	-me	tu	-	hai	-	kan	-dhe	-	pe

N	-	-S'	N	DN	-D	S'	N	P	M*	P	-	-	GG	-P	-D
me	-	- re	-	sr	-ko	-	jhu	ka	-	ye	-	-	mukh	-pe	-I

S'	N	D	P	PM	-	G	M	G	R
ten	-	bi	kh	ra-	-	ye	-	-	-

interlude: RM ND ND RM -2
        GP ND ND GP -2
        N—DNS'G'R'S'N
        S' N--- D N S'
        D N S' N D N S' –

 DDD NN D D DS'N N DN NR'S' S'-R'S' N DD
 mnzil mere dil ki vhin- hai, saya jha-   dildar hai tera

DNR'N R'R'R'R' R'ND ND N-NN NS'N DNDS' N PM*P
prbt   prbt   te-ri bahe, gulshn gulshn pya--r hai te-ra

GGP   D S'NDP PMGMGR   MM   G--
mhke hai aan-chl me-ra-----, mera pyar…

33.   MERE MAHBOOB NA JA

Film: Noor Mahal (1965)   Music: Jaani Babu Kawwal
Lyrics: Saba Afgani   Singer: Suman K.
Taal: Daadra   Actor: Chitra, Jagdip   Chord: RM*D   S=C

aa....aa.....
mere mehboob na ja, na ja na ja
mere mehboob na ja, aaj ki rat na ja
hone wali hai sahar,
thodi der aur thahar
mere mehboob na jaa

dekh kitana hasin mausam hai
har taraf ik ajib aalam hai
zarre is tarah aaj nikhare hai
jaise taare zami pe bikhare hai
jaise taare zami pe bikhare hai
mere mehboob...

maine kaate hai intazaar ke din
tab kahin aaye hain bahaar ke din
yun naa jaa dil ki shamaa gul kar ke
abhi dekha nahi hai ji bhar ke
abhi dekha nahi hai ji bhar ke
mere mehboob.....

jab se zulfon ki chhaon paayi hai
beqaraari ko nind aayi hai
is qayamat ko yun hi sone de
raat dhalne de subaha hone de

raat dhalne de subaha hone de
mere mehboob....

is tarah fer kar nazar mujh se
dur jaayega tu agar mujh se
chandani se bhi aag barsegi
shammaa bhi roshani ko tarsegi
shammaa bhi roshani ko tarsegi
mere mehboob...

dhadkanon me yahi taraane hain
tere rukne ke sau bahaane hain
mere dil ki zara sadaa sun le
pyaasi nazaron ki iltija sun le
pyaasi nazaron ki iltija sun le
mere mehboob...

MERE MAHBOOB NA JA

dhi	na	ti	na	dhi	na	dhi	na	ti	na	dhi	na
1	2	3	4	5	6	1	2	3	4	5	6

prelude:
GM* RG- GM* RG- GM* RG-
M' G' R' S' N D M* G R

DR' S'R' S'R' S'R' M*' G' R' S' D, M*' G' R' S' D
aa- aa- aa- aa-

DS' NS' NS' NS' M*' G' M*', M*' G' M*', M*' G' M*',
aa- aa- aa- aa-

M' G' R' S' N D M* G R

D S'   R' M*' G' M*' --- G' R' S' S'   S'R'
me   re m   h bu ----------b na ja-

N S'R'NS'R'N ---------D   N D M* G M* R
na---------------------ja   na---------ja

M*'G' M*'G' M*'G' M*'G' M*'G' M*'G' M*'G' M*'G'
M*GM*   PM*D--   M*GR

				M*	M*	P	P
				me	re	m	h
M*	-	R	R	G	- R	DM*	D	M*	-	P	-
bu	-	b	n	ja	-	-	-	aa	-j	ki	-
M*	-	R	R	G	-	M*	-	M*	D	N	R'
ra	-	t	n	ja	-	-	-	ho	ne	va	-
S'	-	D	D	N	-	M*	-	M*	D	N	R'
li	-	hai	s	hr	-	-	-	tho	di	de	-r
S'	-	D	D	N	-	M*	-	M*	M*	P	P
au	-	r	th	hr	-	-	-	me	re	m	h
M*	-	R	R	G	-	-	-				
bu	-	b	n	ja	-	-	-				

interlude: P'M'G'R' R'S'ND
M*'G'M*'G'M*'---D'M*'D'M*'D'---
M*' –P'M'P'D' N'D'P'M*'G'R'
N' D' G'M*'G'M*' – G'M*'G'M*'- G'M*'G'M*'-

						R	R	G	G
						de	kh	ki	t
M*	-	M*	M*	-	M*	M*	G	G	P	M*	-
na	-	h	sii	-	n	mau	-	s	m	hai	-

G	R	R	R	G	G	M*	M*	M*	M*	-	M*
-	-	hr	t	r	f	i	k	a	ji	-	b
M*	G	G	P	M*	-	S'R'	G'M*'	M*'	M*'	M*'	M*'
aa	-	l	m	hai	-	-	-	z	rre	i	s
G'	G'	G'	R'	-	S'	S'	R'	R'	-	R'	-
t	r	h	aa	-	j	ni	kh	re	-	hain	-
S'	M*'	M*'	M*'	M*'	-	G'	-	G'	R'	-	S'
-	-	jai	se	ta	-	re	-	z	mi	-	pe
S'	R'	R'	-	R'	-	-	-	S'	S'	S'	N
bi	kh	re	-	hain	-	-	-	jai	se	ta	-
S'	-	N	S'	-	N	N	D	D	-	D	-
re	-	z	mi	-	pe	bi	kh	re	-	hain	-
M*	-	M*	M*	P	P	M*	-	R	R	G	-
-	-	me	re	m	h	bu	-	b	n	ja	-
R	-	M*	-	P	-	M*	-	R	R	G	-
-	-	aa	-j	ki	-	ra	-	t	n	ja	-
M*	-										
aa	-										

interlude:

P'M'G'R' R'S'ND

M*'G'M*'G'M*'---D'M*'D'M*'D'---

M*' –P'M'P'D' N'D'P'M*'G'R'

N' D' G'M*'G'M*' – G'M*'G'M*'- G'M*'G'M*'-

	RR		GM*	M*	M*M*M*GG	P	M*- GR
2) mainne	kate	hain	intzar			ke	din

R   RG   M*M*   M*-M*M*GG   P   M*-   S'R'G'M*'
tb khin aaye hain bha-r   ke din   music

M*' M*'M*' G' G'   R'-S' S'R'   R'   R' – M*'
yu na ja   dil ki shmma gul kr ke

M*'M*'   M*'G'   G'R' S' S'R'   R'   R'
abhi   dekha   nhin hai ji   bhr ke

S'S'   S'NS'   NS' N ND D D –M*
abhi de-kha nhin hai ji- bhr ke,

M*M* PPM*-R R G R
mere   mhbu-b n ja –

    R   R   GM* M*   M*M* M*GGP M* - GR
3) jb se zulfo ki   chhanv pa-ii-   hai

RR GM* M* M*-M* M*GGP M*- G R
beqrari ko nin-d aa-ii-   hai

M*' M*'M*'G'   G'   R'-S' R'R'   R' –S' M*'
is   qyamt   ko yu   hi   sone de

M*'M*'   M*' G' G' R' S' R'R'   R'
rat   dhlne de subh hone de

S'S' S'NS'   N S'N   ND D –M*
rat   dhlne   de subh hone de,

M*M* PPM*-R R G M*
mere mhbu-b n ja –

   R RG M*-M* M* M*M*G GP M* - GR
4) is trh fe-r kr nzr mujh se

RR GM*DM*M* M*- M*M*G GP M*- S'R'G'M*'
dur ja--ega tu agr mujh se

M*'M*'M*' G' G' R'-S' S'R'R'R' –
chandni se bhi aag brsegi

M*'M*' M*' G'G'R' S' S'R'R'R'
shmma bhi roshni ko trsegi

S'S' S'N S'NS' N NDDD –M*
shmma bhi- roshni ko trsegi

M*M* PPM*-R R G –R
mere mhbu-b n ja –

   RRG M* M*M* M*M*GGP M* - GR
5) dhdkno me yhi tra-ne- hain

RR GDPM* M* M*- M*M*GGP M*- NS'R'G'M*'-
tere rukne- ke sau baha-ne- hain

M*'M*' M*' G' R'R' S'S'R' R' R' – M*'
mere dil ki zra sda sun le

M*'M*'   M*'M*'G' G' R'S'S'R'   R'R'   R'
pyasii   nzro   ki   iltja-   sun   le

S'S'   S'NS'   N S'NND   D   D –M*R
pyasii   nzro   ki iltja-   sun   le

M*M* PPM*-R R   G R
mere   mhbu-b n   ja –

34.   MERE SANG GA GUNGUNA

Film: Jaanvar (1965)   Music: Jaikishan
Lyrics: Hasrat Jaipuri   Singer: Suman K.
Taal: Teen Taal   Chord: MDS'   S=D

aa...aa...aa..aa...aa...
mere sang ga gunguna koi giit suhana -2
mere sang ga gunguna

mai bhi tumhari, dil bhi tumahara, mai bhi tumhari
mai bhi tumhari, dil bhi tumahara
sang sath jug jug se hamara -2
tere hi kadmo me sar mera
mere sang ga gunguna koi giit suhana -2
mere sang ga gunguna

shisha e dil me teri suratiya, shisha e dil me
shishaye dil me teri suratiya
dekhun raat din teri muratiya -2
tu mere pyar ka devta
mere sang ga gunguna koi giit suhana -2
mere sang ga gunguna

pahali nazar me apna banaya, pahali nazar me
pahali nazar me apna banaya
tumne pyar se jeena sikhaaya
chhote munh ab tera shukariya
mere sang ga gunguna koi giit suhana -2
mere sang ga gunguna

Vinod Kumar

MERE SANG GA GUNGUNA

dha	dhin	dhin	dha	dha	dhin	dhin	dha	dha	tin	tin	ta	ta	dhin	dhin	dha
1	2	3	4	5	6	7	8	9	10	11	12	13	14	15	16

```
.M.D--------- .N .D .DS----
aa----------------- ---------

S    S G------- G M -----
aa-----------------------

M M N D S' -----   S'---- N D ---- MG ----
aa----------------  aa--------------------

G --- R --- S--- .D S---
aa----------------------

                                      .D  -  S  -  | -  M  -  D
                                      me  -  re  - | -  sn -  g

S'  -   -   -  | -  S'  -  N | D  -  -  -  | -  -  D  D
ga  -   -   -  | -  gun -  gu| na -  -  -  | -  -  ko ii

D   N   D   M  | M  -   R  S
gi  -   t   su | ha -   na -

D    P   D   M  | P   M  D  -  | S'  N  S'  D | N  P  D  -
main -   bhi tu | mha -  ri -  | dil -  bhi tu| mha -  ra -

-    DP  D   P  | D   M  D  -  | -   -  -   - | -  -  -  -
-    main-bhi tu| mha -  ri -  | -   -  -   - | -  -  -  -

D    P   D   M  | P   M  D  -  | S'  N  S'  D | N  P  D  -
main -   bhi tu | mha -  ri -  | dil -  bhi tu| mha -  ra -

DG'  -   R'  S' | -   S' D  P  | S'  N  S'  D | N  P  D  -
sn-  -   g   sa | -   th ju g  | ju  g  se  h | ma -  ra -
```

-	S	.D	S	M	-	-	M	R	M	D	-	-	D	M	D
-	te	-	re	hi	-	-	k	d	mo	me	-	-	s	r	me
M'	-	-	-	-	-	R'	S'	G'	-	-	-	R'	-	S'	-
ra	-	-	-	-	-	-	-	-	-	-	-	-	-	-	-
D	P	D	M	P	M	D	-	S'	N	S'	D	N	P	D	-
shi	-	sha	e	dil	-	me	-	te	-	ri	su	r	ti	ya	-
-	DP	D	M	P	M	D	-	-	-	-	-	-	-	-	-
-	shi-	sha	e	dil	-	me	-	-	-	-	-	-	-	-	-
DG'	-	R'	S'	-	S'	D	P	S'	N	S'	D	N	P	D	-
de-	-	khu	ra	-	t	di	n	te	-	ri	mu	r	ti	ya	-
-	S	.D	S	M	-	-	M	R	M	D	-	-	D	M	D
-	tu	-	me	re	-	-	pya	-	r	ka	-	-	de	-	v
M'	-	-	-	-	-	R'	S'	G'	-	-	-	R'	-	S'	-
ta	-	-	-	-	-	-	-	-	-	-	-	-	-	-	-
D	P	D	M	P	M	D	-	S'	N	S'	D	N	P	D	-
p	h	li	n	z	r	me	-	a	p	na	b	na	-	ya	-
-	DP	D	M	P	M	D	-	-	-	-	-	-	-	-	-
-	ph	li	n	z	r	me	-	-	-	-	-	-	-	-	-
DG'	-	R'	S'	-	S'	D	P	S'	N	S'	D	N	P	D	-
tum	-	ne	pya	-	r	se	-	ji	-	na	si	kha	-	ya	-
-	S	.D	S	M	-	-	M	R	M	D	-	-	D	M	D
-	chho	-	te	muh	-	-	a	b	te	ra	-	-	shu	k	ri
M'	-	-	-	-	-	R'	S'	G'	-	-	-	R'	-	S'	-
ya	-	-	-	-	-	-	-	-	-	-	-	-	-	-	-

35. NA TUM HAME JAANO

Film: Baat Ek Raat Ki (1962)   Music: Hemant Kumar
Lyrics: Majrooh Sultanpuri   Singer: Hemant Kumar, Suman K.
Taal: Kaharwa   Chord: RM<u>N</u> RMD S=C

na tum hamen jaano, na ham tumhen jaane
magar lagata, hai kuchh aisa, mera hamadam, mil gaya

ye mausam ye raat chup hai
wo honthon ki baat chup hai
khaamoshi sunaane lagi hai daastaan
nazar ban gayi hai dil ki zabaan

mohabbat ke mod pe ham
mile sabako chhodke ham
dhadkate dilon ka leke ye kaarawaan
chale aaj donon jaane kahaan

NA TUM HAME JAANO

dha	ge	n	ti	n	ke	dhi	n	dha	ge	n	ti	n	ke	dhi	n
1	2	3	4	5	6	7	8	1	2	3	4	5	6	7	8

prelude: M'- G'- S'- D- N-   MPM- DS'N-

											M	D	S'	N	D
											n	tu	m	h	me
N	D	P	D	N	-	-	-	-	-	-	D	N	S'	N	D
ja	-	-	-	no	-	-	-	-	-	-	n	h	m	tu	mhe
N	D	P	M	D	-	-	-	-	-	-	D	D	D	D	N
ja	-	-	-	ne	-	-	-	-	-	-	m	g	r	l	g
D	P	-	D	D	D	D	N	D	M	-	M	D	-	D	-
ta	-	-	hai	ku	chh	ae	-	sa	-	-	me	ra	-	hm	-
S'	-	-	-	-	G'	-	R'	R'	-	-	-	-	-	-	-
dm	-	-	-	-	mi	l	g	ya	-	-	-	-	-	-	-

interlude:

R' S' R' S' ND P M*-   D- D P M* P- D- N-

P N R' S' N P M*-   D S'M' G'R'S' N-

										N	S'	-	R'	-	S'
										ye	mau	-	sm	-	ye
R'	-	-	S'	R'	G'	N	-	-	-	N	S'	-	R'	-	S'
ra	-	-	t	chu	p	hai	-	-	-	vo	ho	-	tho	-	ki
R'	-	-	S'	R'	G'	N	-	-	-	N	S'	G'	G'	-	R'
ba	-	-	t	chu	p	hai	-	-	-	kha	mo	-	shi	-	su
S'	R'	N	-	-	N	N	-	-	-	R'	-	-	S'	-	S'
na	-	ne	-	-	l	gi	-	-	-	hai	-	-	da	-	s
S'	-	-	-	-		N (R')	-	-	-	D	D	-	D	-	D
ta	-	-	-	-	-	-	-	dh	-	n	zr	-	bn	-	g

N	D	P	N	-	N	-	-	-	-	S'	N	-	S'	N	N
yi	-	-	-	-	hai	-	-	-	-	dil	-	-	ki	-	z

N	-	-	-	D^N	-	P^D	-	M	-	-	M	D	S'	N	D
ba	-	-	-	-	-	-	-	-	-	-	n	tu	m	h	me

N	D	P	D	N	-	-	-	-	-	-	D	N	S'	N	D
ja	-	-	-	no	-	-	-	-	-	-	n	h	m	tu	mhe

N	D	P	M	D	-	-	-	-	-	-	D	D	D	D	N
ja	-	-	-	ne	-	-	-	-	-	-	m	g	r	l	g

D	P	-	D	D	D	D	N	D	M	-	M	D	-	D	-
ta	-	-	hai	ku	chh	ae	-	sa	-	-	me	ra	-	hm	-

S'	-	-	-	-	G'	-	R'	R'	-	-	-	-	-	-	-
dm	-	-	-	-	mi	l	g	ya	-	-	-	-	-	-	-

interlude:

R' S' R' S' ND P M*-   D- D P M* P- D- N-

P N R' S' N P M*-   D S' M' G' R' S' N-

										N	S'	-	R'	-	S'
										mo	ho	-	b	t	ke

R'	-	-	S'	R'	-	N	-	-	-	N	S'	-	R'	-	S'
mo	-	-	d	pe	-	hm	-	-	-	mi	le	-	s	b	ko

R'	-	-	S'	R'	-	N	-	-	-	N	S'	G'	G'	-	R'
chho	-	-	d	ke	-	hm	-	-	-	dh	d	k	te	-	di

S'	R'	N	-	-	N	-	N	-	-	R'	-	-	S'	-	S'
lo	-	ka	-	-	le	-	ke	-	-	ye	-	-	ka	-	r

S'	-	-	-	-	R'	N	-	-	-	D	D	-	D	-	D
va	-	-	-	-	-	-	-	-	-	ch	le	-	aa	-	j

N	D	P	N	-	N	-	-	-	-	S'	N	-	S'	-	N
do	-	-	-	-	no	-	-	-	-	ja	-	-	ne	-	k
N	-	-	-	D^N	-	P^D	-	M	-	-	M	D	S'	N	D
ha	-	-	-	-	-	-	-	-	-	-	n	tum	-	h	me
N	D	P	D	N	-	-	-	-	-	-					
ja	-	-	-	no	-	-	-	-	-	-					

36. NA JAANE KAISE PAL ME BADAL

Film: Badalte Rishte (1978)   Music: Laxmikant Pyarelal
Lyrics: Anjaan   Singer: Suman K. Kishore, Md. Rafi
Taal: Daadra   Chord: M$\underline{D}$S' $\underline{GPN}$ S=C#

Suman:

na jaane kaise pal me badal jaate hain -2

ye duniya ke badalte rishte

kya jaane kaise rangon me dhal jaate hain

ye duniya ke badalte rishte

na jaane kaise pal me badal jaate hain

Kishore:

judkar kahin dil jod dein toote to dil tod jaate hain ye -2

ye phool bankar hain khilte kahin

kahin dil me kaante chubhaate hain ye

jaane kahan kis mod pe de ke daga dil ko chhal jaate hain

ye duniya ke badalte rishte

na jaane kaise pal me badal jaate hain

ye duniya ke badalte rishte

Suman:
(apnon se yoon bichde hain jo
unhen kya bichhadne ka kuch gham nahin) -2
magar haar kar kyun dukhon se koi
jahar ghol de zindagi me kahin
sab khel hai taqdeer ka
taqdeer se hi badal jaate hain
ye duniya ke badalte rishte
na jaane kaise pal me badal jaate hain
ye duniya ke badalte rishte

Md. Rafi
rishte kabhi toote kahan jo toot jaaye wo rishte nahin -2
chhupi hai udaasi ke peeche hansi
dabi dard me bhi khushi hai kahin
sach to hai ye bas pyar se jeewan hamare badal jaate hain
ye duniya ke badalte rishte
na jaane kaise pal me badal jaate hain
ye duniya ke badalte rishte

NA JAANE KAISE PAL ME BADAL

| dha | dhi | na | dha | tun | na | dha | dhi | na | dha | tun | na |
1	2	3	4	5	6	1	2	3	4	5	6
M	-	-	P	D	S'	N	-	-	-	-	-
na	-	-	ja	ne	kai	se	-	-	-	-	-
PM	G	-G	M	P	N	D	-	-	-	-	-
pl	me	-b	dl	ja	te	hain	-	-	-	-	-
G'	-	-	R'	S'	N	N	P	-P	P	D	-
ye	-	-	duni	ya	-	ke	-	-b	dl	te	-
M	M	-	-	-	-	M	-	-	P	D	S'
rish	te	-	-	-	-	kya	-	-	ja	ne	kai
N	-	-	-	-	-	PM	G	G	M	P	N
se	-	-	-	-	-	rn-	go	me	dhl	ja	te
D	-	-	-	-	-	G'	-	-	R'	S'	N
hain	-	-	-	-	-	ye	-	-	duni	ya	-
N	P	-P	P	D	-	M	M	-	-	-	-
ke	-	-b	dl	te	-	rish	te	-	-	-	-
G'	G'	-R'	G'	-	-	S'R'	G'	-R'	S'	-	-
jud	kr	-k	hin	-	-	dil	jo	-d	de	-	-
N	N	-N	S'	S'	-S'	S'R'	G'	-R'	S'	-	-
tu	te	-to	dil	to	-d	ja-	te	-hain	ye	-	-
G'	G'	-R'	G'	G'	-S'	S'	R'	-S'	N	-	-D
ye	fu	-l	bn	kr	-hain	khil	te	-k	hin	-	-k
N	S'	-N	D	N	-P	P	D	-P	M	-	-
hin	dil	-ye	kan	te	-chu	bha	te	-hain	ye	-	-

G	M	-G	M	-	-	MM	P	-M	P	-	-
ja	ne	-k	ha	-	-	kis	mo	-d	pe	-	-
P	P	-D	N	N	N	S'R'	G'	-R'	S'	-	-
de	ke	-d	ga	dil	ko	chhl	ja	-te	hain	-	-
G'	-	-	R'R'	S'	-	N	-	-P	P	D	-
ye	-	-	duni	ya	-	ke	-	-b	dl	te	-
M	M	-	-	-	-	M	-	-	P	D	S'
rish	te	-	-	-	-	na	-	-	ja	ne	kai
N	-	-	-	-	-						
se	-	-	-	-	-						
G'G'	G'	-R'	G'	-	-	S'R'	G'	-R'	S'	-	-D
ap	no	-se	yu	-	-	bichh	de	-hain	jo	-	-u
N	N	-N	NS'	S'	-S'	S'R'	G'	-R'	S'	-	-G'
nhe	kya	-bi	chhd	ne	-ka	kuchh	gm	-n	hin	-	-m
G'G'	G'	-R'	G'	G'	-S'	S'	R'	-S'	N	-	-D
gr	ha	-r	kr	kyu	-du	khon	se	-ko	ii	-	-z
N	S'	-N	D	N	P	P	D	-P	M	-	-
hr	gho	-l	de	zin	-d	gi	me	-k	hin	-	-
GG	M	-G	M	-	-	MM	P	-M	P	-	-
sb	khe	-l	hai	-	-	tq	di	-r	ka	-	-
PP	P	-D	N	N	-N	S'R'	G'	-R'	S'	-	-
tq	di	-r	se	bhi	-b	dl	ja	-te	hain	-	-
G'	-	-	R'R'	S'	-	N	-	-P	P	D	-
ye	-	-	duni	ya	-	ke	-	-b	dl	te	-

M	M	-	-	-	-	M	-	-	P	D	S'
rish	te	-	-	-	-	na	-	-	ja	ne	kai
N	-	-	-	-	-						
se	-	-	-	-	-						
G'	G'	-R'	G'	-	-	S'R'	G'	-R'	S'	-	-
rish	te	-k	bhi	-	-	tu	te	-k	ha	-	-
N	N	-N	S'	S'	-S'	S'R'	G'	-R'	S'	-	-G'
jo	tu	-t	ja	ye	-vo	rish	te	-n	hin	-	chhu
G'	G'	-R'	G'	G'	-S'	S'	R'	-S'	N	-	-D
pi	hai	-u	da	sii	-ke	pi	chhe	-hn	sii	-	-d
N	S'	-N	D	N	P	P	D	-P	M	-	-
bi	d	-rd	me	bhi	-khu	shi	hai	-k	hin	-	-
G	M	-G	M	-	-	MM	P	-M	P	-	-
sch	to	hai	ye	-	-	bs	pya	-r	se	-	-
P	P	-D	N	S'	-S'	S'R'	G'	-R'	S'	-	-
ji	vn	-h	ma	re	-b	dl	ja	-te	hain	-	-
G'	-	-	R'R'	S'	-	N	-	-P	P	D	-
ye	-	-	duni	ya	-	ke	-	-b	dl	te	-
M	M	-	-	-	-	M	-	-	P	D	S'
rish	te	-	-	-	-	na	-	-	ja	ne	kai
N	-	-	-	-	-						
se	-	-	-	-	-						

37. NA NA KARTE PYAR TUMHIN SE

Film: Jab Jab Phool Khile (1965)   Music: Kalyanji Anandji
Lyrics: Anand Bakshi   Singer: Suman K., Md. Rafi
Taal: Kaharwa dugun   Chord: RMD MDS'   S=D

na na karate,
na na karate pyaar tumhin se kar baithe -2
karna tha inkaar magar iqaraar tumhin se kar baithe
na na karate pyaar tumhin se kar baithe -2

dekho ji bhari hain hazaaro tumne aahen
tab kahin hum ne, achaa,
tab kahin hum ne milaai hai nigahen
tum se bhi hasin hai tumhara ye bahana
tumne hi to humko sikhayaa dil lagaana
sikha hai dildaar tumhi se pyaar tumhi se kar bethe
na na karate aaha na na karate pyaar tumhin se kar baithe
karna tha inkaar magar iqaraar tumhin se kar baithe
na na karate pyaar tumhin se kar baithe

ham ko hai pataa jo tumhaari daastaan thi
honthon pe to na thi
honthon pe to na thi jaa juthe
honthon pe to na thi magar dil mein haan thi
koi dil na degaa anaadi anajaan ko
hamane de diyaa hai to maano ehasaan ko
ham bhuule ik baar ki aankhen chaar tumhin se kar baithe
na na karate
na na karate pyaar tumhin se kar baithe
karna tha inkaar magar iqaraar tumhin se kar baithe
na na karate pyaar tumhin se kar baithe

chhodo rahane bhi do ye jhuuthe afasaane

aisa kya hai tum mein chal jhuuthi

aisa kya hai tum mein ki ham hon deewane

phir bhi tumane khwabo mein aanaa nahin chhoda

tir nazaron ke chalana nahin chhoda

ye shiqavaa sarkaar hazaaron baar tumhin se kar baithe

na na karate haan

na na karate pyaar tumhin se kar baithe

karna tha inkaar magar iqaraar tumhin se kar baithe

na na karate pyaar tumhin se kar baithe -2

NA NA KARTE PYAR TUMHIN SE

dhage	nti	nke	dhin	dhage	nti	nke	dhin	dhage	nti	nke	dhin	dhage	nti	nke	dhin
12	34	56	78	12	34	56	78	12	34	56	78	12	34	56	78
prelude: M- DPMGRG M- MM- M-															
M M DP P			MDPDMPM-												
na na krte -----------															
												M	M	DP	P
												na	na	kr	te
M	-G	R	G	D	P	M	-	MD	PD	MP	M-	M	M	DP	P
pya	r,tumhin		se	kr	bai	the	-	-	-	-	-	na	na	kr	te
M	-G	R	G	D	P	M	-	D<u>N</u>	DP	D<u>N</u>	S'-	S'	S'	S'	S'
pya	r,tumhin		se	kr	bai	the	-	-	-	-	-	kr	na	tha	in
S'	S'	S'	S'	S'	-P	P	P	S'	<u>N</u>	D	-	M	M	DP	P
ka	r,m	gr	ik	ra	r,tumhin		se	kr	bai the		-	na	na	kr	te
M	-G	R	G	D	P	M	-								
pya	r,tumhin		se	kr	bai	the	-								
interlude:															

M M M P D D D - D PD<u>N</u>D PMRS S- S- S-
R- RR-G M M M   MPDP MGRG M- M- M-
M M M P D D D - D PD<u>N</u>D PMRS S- S- S-
R- RR-G M M M   D-P MGRS R- G- M-

| | | | <u>N</u> | <u>N</u> | R' | R' |
| | | | de | kho | ji | bh |

| R' | - | R' | R' | R' | <u>G'</u> | R' | S' | S' | - | S' | - | <u>N</u> | <u>N</u> | R' | - |
| ri | - | hain | h | za | ro | tum | ne | aa | - | he | - | tb | k | hin | - |

| R' | - | R' | R' | R' | <u>G'</u> | R' | S' | S' | - | S' | - | <u>N</u> | <u>N</u> | <u>N</u> | <u>N</u> |
| hm | - | ne | mi | la | ii | hain | ni | ga | - | hen | - | tum | se | bhi | hn |

| D | - | D | D | <u>N</u> | <u>N</u> | <u>N</u> | <u>N</u> | D | - | D | - | <u>N</u> | <u>N</u> | <u>N</u> | <u>N</u> |
| sii | - | hain tum | ha | ra | ye | b | ha | - | na | - | tum | ne | hi | to |

| D | - | D | D | <u>N</u> | R' | S' | <u>N</u> | D | - | D | S' | S' | S' | S' | S' |
| hm | - | ko | l | ga | ya | dil | l | ga | - | na | - | sii | kha | hai | dil |

| S' | -S' | S' | S' | S' | -P | P | P | S' | <u>N</u> | D | - | P | - | M | - |
| dar | -tu | mhin | se | pya | r,tumhin | se | kr | bai the | - | e | - | e | - |

| M | M | DP | P | MD | PD | MP | M- | M | M | DP | P | M | -G | R | G |
| na | na | kr | te | - | - | - | - | na | na | kr | te | pya | r,tu | mhin | se |

| D | P | M | - |
| kr | bai | the | - |

interlude: S' <u>N</u> D P M G S -
S- G------ RGRGRG--- 2
G- P------- PDPDP--- 2
R'- S'—D—P <u>N</u>- D—PDM--- 2

| | | | <u>N</u> | <u>N</u> | R' | R' |
| | | | hm | ko | hai | p |

| R' | - | R' | R' | R' | <u>G'</u> | R' | S' | S' | - | S' | - | <u>N</u> | <u>N</u> | R' | R' |
| ta | - | jo tum | ha | ri | da | s | ta | - | thi | - | ho | to | pe | to |

R'	-R'	-	-	D	-	-	D	R'	-	-	-	N	N	R'	R'
na	thi	-	-	ja	-	-	jhu	te	-	-	-	ho	to	pe	to
R'	-R'	-	R'	R'	G'	R'	S'	S'	-	S'	-	N	N	N	N
na	thi	-	m	g	r	dil	me	ha	-	thi	-	ko	ii	dil	na
D	-	D	D	N	N	N	-	D	-	D	-	N	N	N	N
de	-	ta	a	na	di	an	-	ja	-n	ko	-	hm	ne	de	di
D	-	D	D	N	R'	S'	N	D	-	D	S'	S'	S'	S'	S'
ya	-	hai	to	ma	no	e	h	sa	-n	ko	-	hm	bhu	le	ik
S'	-S'	S'	S'	S'	-P	P	P	S'	N	D	-				
ba	r,ki	aan	khe	chhar,	tumhin	se		kr	bai	the	-				

38. PARBATON KE PEDON PAR

Film: Shagun (1964)   Music: khaiyyam
Lyrics: Sahir Ludhiyanvi   Singer: Md. Rafi, Suman K.
Taal: Daadra   Chord: MDR' S=C#

R: parbaton ke pedon par shaam ka basera hai -2
      suramayi ujala hai champayi andhera hai -2

S: dono waqt milate hai do dilo ki surat se -2
      aasma ne khush hoke rang saa bikheraa hai -2

R: thahare thahare paani me git sar saraate hai -2
      bhige bhige jhokon me khushbuon ka dera hai -2
      parbaton ke pedon par

S: kyo na jazb ho jaayein is haseen nazaare me -2
      roshani ka jhuramat hai mastiyo ka ghera hai -2
      parbaton ke pedon par

R: ab kisi nazaare ki dil ko aarzu kyon ho -2
      jab se pa liya tum ko sab jahaan mera hai -2

B: jab se pa liya tum ko sab jahaan mera hai
      parbaton ke pedon par shaam ka basera hai
      parbaton ke pedon par.

PARBATON KE PEDON PAR

dhin	dhin	na	ti	dhin	na	dhin	dhin	na	ti	dhin	na	dhin	dhin	na	ti	dhin	na
1	2	3	4	5	6	1	2	3	4	5	6	1	2	3	4	5	6
														D	D	D	D
														p	rb	to	ke
P	-	M	-	M	-	-	-	M	-P	P	P	ᴰP	-	P	D	D	-
pe	-	do	-	pr	-	-	-	sha	-m	ka	b	se	-	ra	-	hai	-
Pᴹ	-	D	D	D	D	P	-	M	-	M	-	-	-	M	-P	P	P
-	-	p	rb	to	ke	pe	-	do	-	pr	-	-	-	sha	-m	ka	b
ᴰP	-	P	D	D	-	P	-	D	D	D	D	P	-	M	-	M	-
se	-	ra	-	hai	-	-	-	sur	m	yi	u	ja	-	la	-	hai	-
-	-	M	P	P	P	P	-	P	D	D	-	-	-	D	D	D	D
-	-	chn	p	yi	an	dhe	-	ra	-	hai	-	-	-	sur	m	yi	u
P	-	M	-	M	-	-	-					-	-	D	D	D	D
ja	-	la	-	hai	-	-	-					-	-	do	no	v	qt
P	-	M	-	M	-	-	-	M	P	P	P	ᴰP	-	P	D	D	-
mil	-	te	-	hain	-	-	-	do	di	lo	ki	su	-	r	t	se	-
Pᴹ	-	D	D	D	D	P	-	M	-	M	-	-	-	M	P	P	P
-	-	do	no	v	qt	mil	-	te	-	hain	-	-	-	do	di	lo	ki
ᴰP	-	P	D	D	-	-	-	D	-D	D	D	P	P	M	-	M	-
su	-	r	t	se	-	-	-	aa	-s	ma	ne	khu	sh	ho	-	kr	-
-	-	M	P	P	P	ᴰP	-	P	D	D	-	Pᴹ	-	D	-D	D	D
-	-	rn	g	sa	bi	khe	-	ra	-	hai	-	-	-	aa	-s	ma	ne
P	P	M	-	M	-	-	-										
khu	sh	ho	-	kr	-	-	-										

		R' -	S' N	D -	P -	D -	- -	D D	D D	D D	D -	D -	N -

```
                                          D  D | D  D | D  -  | D  -  | N  -
                                          thh re| thh re| pa -  | ni -  | me -

-  -  | R' -  | S' N | D  -  | P  -  | D  -  | -  -  | D  D | D  D
-  -  | gi -t | sr s | ra -  | te -  | hain -| -  -  | thh re| thh re

D  -  | D  -  | N  -  | -  -  | R' -  | S' N | D  -  | P  -  | D  -
pa -  | ni -  | me -  | -  -  | gi -t | sr s | ra -  | te -  | hain -

-  -  | D  D | D  D | P  -  | M  -  | M  -  | -  -  | M  P | P  P
-  -  | bhi ge| bhi ge| jho - | ko -  | me -  | -  -  | khush bu| on ka

Dp -  | P  D | D  -  | PM -  | D  D | D  D | P  -  | M  -  | M  -
de -  | ra -  | hai - | -  -  | bhige | bhi ge| jho - | ko -  | me -

-  -  | M  P | P  P | Dp -  | P  D | D  -  | PM -  | D  D | D  D
-  -  | khush bu| on ka| de -  | ra -  | hai - | -  -  | p rb | to ke

P  -  | M  -  | M  -  | -  -
pe -  | do -  | pr -  | -  -
```

```
D  D  D D D   DNN  D R'S'  NDP   D-P
kyu n  jzb ho ja-en is hsi nzare me

D D D   D  PPMM  M  MPP    P  P-  PD    D
roshni ka jhurmt hai mstiyon ka ghe-ra-  hai

D  DD   DDN  N  D  R'  S'ND   P   D-P
ab kisii nzare ki dil ko aarzu kyu ho

P  D  D  DP  M  M  M  PPP   P-  PD  D-P
jb se pa liya tum ko sb jahan me-ra- hai

D  D  D  DP  M  M  M  PPP   P-  PD  D-P
jb se pa liya tum ko sb jahan me-ra- hai
```

39. PAHLA PAHLA PYAR HAI YE

Film: Badtameez (1966)   Music: Shanker Jaikishan
Lyrics: Shailendra   Singer: Suman K.
Taal: Kaharwa   Chord: SGP   S=C#

ho pahla pahla pyaar hai ye pahla pahla pyaar -2
kya jaane kya ho gaya hai dil hai beqaraar-2
ho pahla pahla pyaar hai ye pahla pahla pyaar -2

(kaate jaise bichhua kuchh aisa mera haal
dil mera bole ke khud ko sambhal) -2
aaj mujhe khud par nahin hai ikhtiyaar -2
pahla pahla pyaar hai ye pahla pahla pyaar

(sharmo haya se hua hai mukh laal
pyaar ne kisi ke ye kar diya kamaal) -2
ang mora sulge ke jaise ho bukhaar -2
pahla pahla pyaar hai ye pahla pahla pyaar

(ghadi ghadi toote ye phool sa badan
rom rom phadke hai kaisi ye chubhan) -2
haay mera aanchal ude hai baar baar -2
pahla pahla pyaar hai ye pahla pahla pyaar

PAHLA PAHLA PYAR HAI YE

dha	ge	n	ti	n	ke	dhi	n	dha	ge	n	ti	n	ke	dhi	n
1	2	3	4	5	6	7	8	1	2	3	4	5	6	7	8
prelude:															
PPS'S' N- N- D- D- P-															
PPDD P- P- G- M- P-															
PPS'S' N- N- D- D- P-															
PPDD P- P- G- G- S-															
														S'	-
														ha	-
S'	-	S'	-	N	-	N	-	P	-	-	-	P	-	D	-
p	h	la	-	p	h	la	-	pya	-	-	r	hai	-	ye	-
M	-	M	-	G	-	G	-	P	-	-	-	-	-	-	-
p	h	la	-	p	h	la	-	pya	-	-	r	-	-	-	-
S	-	G	-	S	-	S	-	P	-	-	M	G	-	G	-
kya	-	ja	-	ne	-	kya	-	ho	-	-	g	ya	-	hai	-
M	D	D	-	D	-	P	-	P	-	-	-	-	D	S'	-
di	l	hai	-	be	-	q	-	ra	-	-	r	-	ho	o	-
interlude:															
P'M*' P'M*' P'D'P'M' G'R' G'R' G'M'G'R' R'S' R'S' R'G'R'S'															
R'S'G'M'P'---															
P- S'- NS' NS' NS' NS'															
P- G'- R'G' R'G' R'G' R'G'															
P'M'G'R'S'NDPDNS'- PMGS-															
		S	-	S	G	-	M	P	-	P	P	-	-	P	-
		ka	-	te	jai	-	se	bi	-	chhu	va	-	-	ku	chh
P	-	P	-	M	-	M	-	G	-	-	-	-	-	-	-
ae	-	sa	-	me	-	ra	-	ha	-	-	-	-	l	-	-

- - M -	- D D -	D - - D	- - N -
- - di l	- me ra -	bo - - le	- - ke -
S' - N -	S' - D -	P - - -	- - - -
khu - d -	ko - sn -	bha - - -	- -l - -
- - P -	P N S' -	R' - - R'	- - R' -
- - aa -	j mu jhe -	khu d - pr	- - n -
N - P -	N - S' -	R' - - -	- - - -
hin - hai -	i kh ti -	ya - - -	- -r - -
- - S' -	S' R' G' -	R' G' - R'	- - S' -
- - aa -	j mu jhe -	khu d - pr	- - n -
S' - S' -	S' - S' -	R' - S' -	N - P -
hin - hai -	i kh ti -	ya - - -	- - - -r

```
  SSG      MP   P  PP   P   MM    G
(shrmo   hya  se  huaa  hai  mukh  lal

  M    D   DD   D   N   S'  NS'  DP
pyar  ne  kisii  ke  ye  kr  diya  kmal) -2

PP     NS'   R'R'   R'  NP   N   S'R'
ang   mora  sulge  ke  jaise  ho  bukhar

S'S'  R'G'   R'G'R'  S'  S'S'  S'  S'R' S' N P
ang   mora  sulge  ke  jaise  ho  bukha------r

S'S'   NN   P   P   D   MM   GG   P
phla  phla  pyar  hai  ye,  phla  phla  pyar
```

40. PAANI ME JALE MERA GORA

Film: Muneem Ji (1955)　　　　Music: Usha Khanna
Lyrics: Neeraj, Hasrat Jaipuri　　Singer: Suman K.
Taal: Kaharwa　　　　　　　　　Chord: P$\underline{N}$R'   S=C#

pani mein jale, pani mein jale mera gora badan pani mein
mere badan ki jwala se lahro mein dekho kaisi lagi agan
lagi agan pani mein
pani mein jale, pani mein jale mera gora badan pani mein

dekho-- thandi thandi aag ye sataye
aaye-- aake koi aag ye bujhaye
jalun main jale dil jale jaan haye re
pani mein jale, pani mein jale mera gora badan pani mein

aaya-- kal koi sapno mein aaya
aake-- aake mujhe usne jagaya
bola main, tere liye aaya hun haye re
pani mein jale, pani mein jale mera gora badan pani mein

PAANI ME JALE MERA GORA

dha	-	-	te	dhin	-	dhin	dhin	dha	-	-	te	dhin	-	dhin	dhin
1	2	3	4	5	6	7	8	1	2	3	4	5	6	7	8
P	D	D	P	M	-	-	-	P	D	D	P	S'	-	D	D
pa	ni	me	j	le	-	-	-	pa	ni	me	j	le	-	me	ra
P	D	-	D	P	-	P	-	M	-	P	-	-	-	-	-
go	ra	-	b	d	n	pa	-	ni	-	me	-	-	-	-	-
S'	R'	-	S'	R'	-	G'	-	S'	R'	S'	N	S'	-	-	-
me	re	-	b	d	n	ki	-	jwa	-	la	-	me	-	-	-
S'	S'	S'	N	S'	R'	R'	S'	N	-S'	-	D	N	-	-	-
l	h	ro	me	de	kho	kai	sii	la	-gi	-	a	gn	-	-	-
D	-P	-	D	D	-	P	-	M	-	P	-	-	-	-	-
la	-gi	-	a	gn	-	pa	-	ni	-	me	-	-	-	-	-
P	-	N	-	-	-	-	-	R'	R'	S'	S'	N	N	D	P
de	-	kho	-	-	-	-	-	thn	di	thn	di	aa	-g	ye	s
D	N	-	-	-	-	-	-	M	-	D	-	-	-	-	-
ta	ye	-	-	-	-	-	-	aa	-	ye	-	-	-	-	-
R'	R'	S'	S'	N	-N	D	P	M	P						
aa	ke	ko	ii	aa	-g	ye	bu	jha	ye	-	-	-	-	-	-
N	D	N	-	N	D	N	-	N	D	N	-	P	-	P	M
j	lu	main	-	j	le	dil	-	j	le	jan	-	ha	-	ye	re
P	D	D	P	M	-	-	-	P	D	D	P	S'	-	D	D
pa	ni	me	j	le	-	-	-	pa	ni	me	j	le	-	me	ra
P	D	-	D	P	-	P	-	M	-	P	-	-	-	-	-
go	ra	-	b	d	n	pa	-	ni	-	me	-	-	-	-	-

```
PN--   R'R'   S'S'   NND    P    DN
aaya-- kl     koii   spno   me   aaya


 MD--   R'R'    S'S'    NND  PMP
aake – aake   mujhe   usne   jgaya


ND     N    ND   NN  ND    N   PP   M
bola  main, tere lie  aaya  hu  hay  re
```

41.   RAHE N RAHE HAM MAHKA

Film: Mamta (1966)   Music: Raushan
Lyrics: Majrooh Sultanpuri   Singer: Lata, Suman K.
Taal: Kaharwa   Chord: RPN   S=C#
Lata:

rahein na rahein hum, mahaka karenge

ban ke kali, ban ke saba, baag e wafaa mein

rahein na rahein hum

mausam koi ho is chaman me rang banke rahenge ham khirama

chahat ki khushabu, yu hi zulfo se udegi, khiza hon ya baharaan

yuhi jhumate, yuhi jhumate aur khilate rahenge

ban ke kali, ban ke saba, baag e wafaa mein

rahe na rahe hum....

khoye ham aise kya hai milna kya bichhadna nahi hai, yad hamko

kunche me dil ke jab se aaye sirf dil ki zami hai, yad hamko

isi sarzami, isi sarzami pe ham to rahenge

ban ke kali, ban ke saba, bage wafaa mein

rahe na rahe hum...

jab ham na hoge tab hamari khak pe tum rukoge chalte chalte

ashqon se bhigi chadani mein ik sada si sunoge chalte chalte

vahi pe kahi, vahi pe kahi ham tumse milenge

ban ke kali, ban ke saba, bage wafaa mein

rahe na rahe hum, mahaka karenge

ban ke kali, ban ke saba, bage wafaa mein

rahe na rahe hum....

Duet Version:

Suman: hai khubsurat ye nazaare, ye bahaarein

              hamare dam qadam se

Md. Rafi: zinda hui hai fir jahaan mein,

              aaj ishq aur vafa ki rasm ham se

Both: yun hi is chaman, yun hi is chaman ki

              zeenat raheinge ban ke kali ban ke saba

              baag e vafa mein,

              rahein na rahein ham.....

RAHE N RAHE HAM MAHKA

dha	ge	n	ti	n	ke	dhi	n	dha	ge	n	ti	n	ke	dhi	n
1	2	3	4	5	6	7	8	1	2	3	4	5	6	7	8
											R	R	G	.N	S
											r	he	–	n	r
R	–	–	N	–	–	–	–	–	–	–	N	–	S′	–	R′
he	–	–	hm	–	–	–	–	–	–	–	m	h	ka	–	k
R′	G′	–	S′	N	–	D	–	–	–	–	D	–	N	–	S′
ren	–	–	–	ge	–	–	–	–	–	–	b	n	ke	–	k
N	–	–	P	–	D	–	N	D	–	–	M*	–	P	–	D
li	–	–	bn	–	ke	–	s	ba	–	–	ba	–	ge	–	v

P	-	-	M*	D	P	M*	G	R	-	-	R	R	G	.N	S
fa	-	-	-	me	-	-	-	-	-	-	r	he	-	n	r
R	-	-	N												
he	-	-	hm												
											N	-	S'	-	N
											mau	-	sm	-	ko
D	N	N	-	-	N	-	D	P	D	D	-	-	D	-	P
ii	-	ho	-	-	i	s	ch	mn	-	me	-	-	rn	-	g
G	P	P	-	-	D	N	-	D	-	-	-	-	D	-	N
bn	-	ke	-	-	r	hen	-	ge	-	-	-	-	hm	-	khi
N	-	P	-	P	-	-	-	-	-	-	N	-	S'	-	N
ra	-	-	-	ma	-	-	-	-	-	-	chha	-	ht	-	ki
D	N	N	-	-	N	-	D	P	D	D	-	-	D	-	P
khu	sh	bu	-	-	yu	-	hi	zu	l	fo	-	-	se	-	u
G	P	P	-	-	D	N	-	D	-	D	-	-	D	-	N
de	-	gi	-	-	khi	za	-	ho	-	ya	-	-	ho	-	b
N	-	P	-	P	-	-	-	-	-	P	D	-	N	R'	N
ha	-	-	-	ra	-	-	-	-	-	yu	hi	-	jhu	-	m
R'	-	-	-	-	-	-	-	-	-	M'	G'	-	R'	-	N
te	-	-	-	-	-	-	-	-	-	yu	hi	-	jhu	-	m
R'	-	-	D	S'	-	N	N	-	-	-	N	-	S'	-	R'
te	-	-	-	aa	-	-	j	-	-	-	khi	l	te	-	r
R'	G'	-	S'	N	-	D	-	-	-	-	D	-	N	-	S'
he	-	-	-	ge	-	-	-	-	-	-	b	n	ke	-	k

N	-	-	P	-	D	-	N	D	-	-	M*	-	P	-	D
li	-	-	bn	-	ke	-	s	ba	-	-	ba	-	ge	-	v

P	-	-	M*	D	P	M*	G	R	-	-	R	R	G	.N	S
fa	-	-	-	me	-	-	-	-	-	-	r	he	-	n	r

R	-	-	N
he	-	-	hm

```
                N   S'NDNN      N   DPDD
      suman:  hai khubsu-rt    ye nza-re


            D   PGPP      DN-D   D  NNP  P
            ye bharen   hma-re  dm-qdm se


                NS'  NDN       N  N  DPD  D
      md. rafi:  zinda huii-    hai fir jha- me


            DP  GP  P DN D  DN  NP  P
            aaj ishq-o-vfa ki rsm hm se


          P  D N   NR'   M' G'  R' NR'D S'N
      dono:  yu hi  is chmn, yu hi  is chmn ki-


            NS'    R' R'G'S'ND
            zint  rhe-----ge-

  '

            D   N  S'N  P  D  ND  M*  P DPM*  DPM*GR
            bn ke kli  bn ke sba  bag-e-vfa     me-----


            RR  G   .NSR     N
            rhe na  rhe-     hm ...
```

42.   THAHARIYE HOSH ME AA LU

Film: Mohobbat isko kahte hain (1965)   Music: Khaiyyam
Lyrics: Majrooh Sultanpuri   Singer: Md. Rafi Suman K.
Taal: Kaharwa   Chord: SGP   S=D

R: thahariye hosh mein aa loo, to chale jaaiyega

S: uun huun

R: aap ko dil mein bithhaa loo to chale jaaiyega

S: uun huun

R: aap ko dil mein bithhaa loo to chale jaaiyega

R: kab talak rahiyega yoon door kee chaahat ban ke -2

        dil mein aa jaaeeye, iqaraar-e-mohabbat ban ke

        apanee taqadeer banaa loo, to chale jaaiyega

S: uun huun

R: aap ko dil mein bithhaa loo to chale jaaiyega

S: mujh ko iqaraar-e-mohabbat pe hayaa aatee hai -2

        baat kahate huye gardn meree jhuk jaatee hai

        dekhiye sar ko jhukaa loon, to chale jaaiyega

R: uun huun

S: dekhiye sar ko jhuka lun to chale jaaiyega

R: aap ko dil mein bithhaa loo to chale jaaiyega

R: aesee kyaa sharm zaraa, paas to aane dije -2

        rukh se bikharee huyee julfein to hataane dije

        pyaas aankhon kee bujhaa loo, to chale jaaiyega

Both: thahariye hosh mein aa loo, to chale jaaiyega

THAHARIYE HOSH ME AA LUN

dha	ge	n	ti	n	ke	dhi	n	dha	ge	n	ti	n	ke	dhi	n
1	2	3	4	5	6	7	8	1	2	3	4	5	6	7	8

prelude: S'NS'R'S'N NDNS'ND DPDNDP P-

dha	ge	n	ti	n	ke	dhi	n	dha	ge	n	ti	n	ke	dhi	n
											P	P	N	D	N
											th	h	ri	ye	-
P	-	-	-	G	G	R	-	G	-	-	-	G	P	DN	S'
ho	-	-	-	sh	me	aa	-	lu	-	-	-	to	ch	le-	-
D	-	D	P	ᴾD	-	D	P	N	-	-	P	-	N	D	N
ja	ii	ye	-	ga	-	un	-	hu	-	-	aa	-	p	ko	-
P	-	P	G	-	G	R	-	G	-	-	-	G	P	DN	S'
dil	-	me	-	-	bi	tha	-	lu	-	-	-	to	ch	le-	-
D	-	D	P	ᴾD	-	D	P	N	-	-	P	-	N	D	N
ja	ii	ye	-	ga	-	un	-	hu	-	-	aa	-	p	ko	-
P	-	P	G	-	G	R	-	G	-	-	-				
dil	-	me	-	-	bi	tha	-	lu	-	-	-				

interlude: RGPDNS' D-D̲D- DDNDPDG G-RG RGPGRGS
sarangi: ND DP GD̲

dha	ge	n	ti	n	ke	dhi	n	dha	ge	n	ti	n	ke	dhi	n
											D̲	D̲	D̲	D̲	D̲
											k	b	t	l	k
D	D	D	-	-	D̲	D	-	DN	S'	-	-	D	D	D	D̲
r	hi	ye	-	-	ga	yu	-	du-	-	-	-	r	ki	chha	-
D	D	D	D̲	N	P	G	-	-	-	-	D̲	-	D̲	D̲	-
h	t	b	n	ke	-	-	-	-	-	-	dil	-	me	aa	-
D	-	-	D	D	-	D	D	DN	S'	-	-	D	D	D	-
ja	-	-	ii	ye	-	i	q	ra-	-	-	-	re	mo	ho	-

D	D	D	D	N	P	G	-	-	-	-	P	P	N	D	N
b	t	b	n	ke	-	-	-	-	-	-	a	p	ni	t	q
P	-	-	-	G	G	R	-	G	-	-	-	G	P	DN	S'
di	-	-	-	r	b	na	-	lu	-	-	-	to	ch	le	-
D	-	D	P	^PD	-	D	P	N	-	-	P	-	N	D	N
ja	ii	ye	-	ga	-	un	-	hu	-	-	aa	-	p	ko	-
P	-	P	G	-	G	R	-	G	-	-	-				
dil	-	me	-	-	bi	tha	-	lu	-	-	-				

interlude: RGPDNS' D-D̲D- DDNDPDG G-RG RGPGRGS
ND DP GD̲

												D̲	D̲	D̲	D̲	D̲
												mu	jh	ko	i	q
D	-	D	-	-	D	D	-	DN	S'	-	-	D	D	D	-
ra	-	re	-	-	mo	ho	-	b-	-	-	t	se	h	ya	-
D	-	D	-	N	P	G	-	-	-	-	D̲	-	D̲	D̲	D̲
aa	-	ti	-	hai	-	-	-	-	-	-	ba	-	t	k	h
D	-	-	D	D	-	D	D	DN	S'	-	-	D	D	D	D
te	-	-	hu	e	-	g	r	dn-	-	-	-	me	ri	jhu	k
D	-	D	-	N	P	G	-	-	-	-	P	-	N	D	N
ja	-	ti	-	hai	-	-	-	-	-	-	de	-	khi	ye	-
P	-	-	-	G	G	R	-	G	-	-	-	G	P	DN	S'
sr	-	-	-	ko	jhu	ka	-	lu	-	-	-	to	ch	le	-
D	-	D	P	^PD	-										
ja	i	ye	-	ga	-										

43.   TUJHE PYAR KARTE HAIN

Film: April Phool (1964)   Music: Shanker Jaikishan
Lyrics: Hasrat Jaipuri   Singer: Md. Rafi, Suman K.
Taal: Kaharwa   Chord: RM*D M*D<u>R</u>'   S=C#

R: tujhe pyaar karte hain karte rahenge
       ke dil banke dil me dhadakte rahenge
S: tera naam le le ke jeete rahenge
       tera naam le le ke marte rahenge
R: tujhe pyaar karte hain karte rahenge
       ke dil banke dil mein dhadakte rahenge

R: tujhe bhool jaaun ye mumkin nahin hai
       kahin bhi rahoon mera dil to yahin hain
       ghate chand lekin mujhe gham na hoga
       tera pyaar dil se kabhi kam na hoga
       guzarne ko ye din guzarte rahenge
       ke dil ban ke di me dhadakte rahenge
S: tera naam le le ke jeete rahenge
       tera naam le le ke marte rahenge
R: tujhe pyaar karte hain karte rahenge
       ke dil banke dil me dhadakte rahenge

S: haseen phool ki zindgaani bhi kya hai
       abhi hans raha tha abhi ro raha hai
       jo guzre khushi me wahi zindagi hai
       nahin to ye duniya badi besuri hai
       teri dhun me bante swarte rahenge
       ke dil banke dil me dhadakte rahenge
S: tera naam le le ke jeete rahenge
       tera naam le le ke marte rahenge

R: tujhe pyaar karte hain karte rahenge

      ke dil banke dil me dhadakte rahenge

R: agar mar gaya rooh aaya karegi

      tujhe dekh kar geet gaaya karegi

      mujhe dekh kar tum na aansoo bahaana

      bas itni guzaarish hai tum muskuraana

      tere pyar me rang bharte rahenge

      ke dil banke dil me dhadakte rahenge

S: tera naam le le ke jeete rahenge

      tera naam le le ke marte rahenge

R: tujhe pyar karte hain karte rahenge

      ke dil banke dil me dhadakte rahenge

TUJHE PYAR KARTE HAIN

dha	ge	n	ti	n	ke	dhi	n	dha	ge	n	ti	n	ke	dhi	n
1	2	3	4	5	6	7	8	1	2	3	4	5	6	7	8

prelude: sitar:

G'- R'G' R'G'M*'G' R' N - 2

G'- R'- N- R' R' R' D R' N R' D D -2

flute: D D D --- M* M* D M* D – G GM* GM*- R- G- -2

synthe: DNR'R' M*' G' R' -2   M*DDN R'- N- D- -2

RGM*D D- D M*- G

D D M*- G- G-

															G -
															tu -
G	-	-	M*	-	-	G	-	G	-	-	M*	-	-	G	-
jhe	-	-	pya	-	-	r	-	k	r	-	te	-	-	hain	-

G	-	-	M*	-	-	G	-	M*	D	-	D	-	-	D	-
k	r	-	te	-	-	r	-	hen	-	-	ge	-	-	ke	-

N	D	-	D	-	-	M*	-	M*	G	-	G	-	-	R	-
dil	-	-	bn	-	-	ke	-	dil	-	-	me	-	-	dh	-

M*	M*	-	M*	-	-	G	-	G	-	-	G	-	-	G'	-
d	k	-	te	-	-	r	-	hen	-	-	ge	-	-	te	-

G'	-	-	R'	N	-	N	-	N	R'	-	R'	-	-	R'	-
ra	-	-	na	-	-	m	-	le	-	-	le	-	-	ke	-

R'	-	-	N	-	-	D	-	N	-	-	D	-	-	D	-
ji	-	-	te	-	-	r	-	hen	-	-	ge	-	-	te	-

D	N	-	D	-	-	M*	-	M*	-	-	G	-	-	R	-
ra	-	-	na	-	-	m	-	le	-	-	le	-	-	ke	-

R	M*	-	M*	-	-	G	-	G	-	-	G	-	-		
m	r	-	te	-	-	r	-	hen	-	-	ge	-	-		

interlude: flute:

R' R' R' R' R'M*' M*'-   G'- G'R'- R' R'-

R' R'M*' M*' G'- G'R'- R' R'-

R' R' M*'- G'M*'- G'M*'-

M*' M*'D' D' P'- P'M*'- M*'G'-   M*' M*'D' D' P'- P'M*'- M*'G'-

D'P'M*'G'-

synthe: R'- R'G' R'N R'N R' D-   R'N R'N R' D R'-

														D	-
														tu	

R'	-	-	R'	-	-	R'	-	R'	-	-	R'	-	-	R'	-
jhe	-	-	bhu	-	-	l	-	ja	-	-	un	-	-	ye	-

R'	-	-	R'	-	-	R'	-	N	R'	-	R'	D	-	D	-
mu	m	-	kin	-	-	n	-	hin	-	-	hai	-	-	k	-

R'	-	-	R'	-	-	R'	-	R'	-	-	R'	-	-	R'	-
hin	-	-	bhi	-	-	r	-	hu	-	-	me	-	-	ra	-
R'	-	-	N	-	-	D	-	R'	-	-	R'	-	-	G'	-
dil	-	-	to	-	-	y	-	hin	-	-	hai	-	-	gh	-
G'	-	-	R'	-	-	N	-	R'	-	-	R'	-	-	R'	-
te	-	-	chan	-	-	d	-	le	-	-	kin	-	-	mu	-
R'	-	-	N	-	-	D	-	N	-	-	D	-	-	D	-
jhe	-	-	gm	-	-	n	-	ho	-	-	ga	-	-	te	-
N	-	-	D	-	-	M*	-	M*	-	-	G	-	-	R	-
ra	-	-	pya	-	-	r	-	dil	-	-	se	-	-	k	-
M*	-	-	M*	-	-	G	-	G	-	-	G	-	-	G	-
bhi	-	-	km	-	-	n	-	ho	-	-	ga	-	-	gu	-
G	-	-	M*	-	-	G	-	G	-	-	M*	-	-	G	-
z	r	-	ne	-	-	ko	-	ye	-	-	din	-	-	gu	-
G	-	-	M*	-	-	G	-	M*	D	-	D	-	-	D	-
z	r	-	te	-	-	r	-	hen	-	-	ge	-	-	ke	-
N	-	-	D	-	-	M*	-	M*	-	-	G	-	-	R	-
dil	-	-	bn	-	-	ke	-	dil	-	-	me	-	-	dh	-
R	M*	-	M*	-	-	G	-	G	-	-	G	-	-		
d	k	-	te	-	-	r	-	hen	-	-	ge	-	-		

interlude: sitar

M* D D N R' R'   G' G' R' N R'

M* D D N R' R'   G' G' R' N R' R' R'

N R' R'   M*' G' R' D N R'   R' R' N

D D N R' N D   R' N D D –

														D	-
														hn	-
R'	-	-	R'	-	-	R'	-	R'	-	-	R'	-	-	G'	-
sii	-	-	fu	-	-	I	-	ki	-	-	zin	-	-	d	-
R'	-	-	R'	-	-	R'	-	N	R'	-	R'	D	-	D	-
ga	-	-	ni	-	-	bhi	-	kya	-	-	hai	-	-	a	-
R'	-	-	R'	-	-	R'	-	R'	-	-	R'	-	-	R'	-
bhi	-	-	hn	-	s	r	-	ha	-	-	tha	-	-	a	-
R'	-	-	N	-	-	D	-	R'	-	-	R'	-	-	G'	-
bhi	-	-	ro	-	-	r	-	ha	-	-	hai	-	-	jo	-
G'	-	-	R'	-	-	N	-	R'	-	-	R'	-	-	R'	-
gu	z	-	re	-	-	khu	-	shi	-	-	me	-	-	v	-
R'	-	-	N	-	-	D	-	N	-	-	D	-	-	D	-
hi	-	-	zin	-	-	d	-	gi	-	-	hai	-	-	n	-
N	-	-	D	-	-	M*	-	M*	G	-	G	-	-	R	-
hin	-	-	to	-	-	ye	-	du	ni	-	ya	-	-	b	-
M*	-	-	M*	-	-	G	-	G	-	-	G	-	-	G	-
di	-	-	be	-	-	su	-	ri	-	-	hai	-	-	te	-
G	-	-	M*	-	-	G	-	G	-	-	M*	-	-	G	-
ri	-	-	dhun	-	-	me	-	bn	-	-	te	-	-	sn	-
G	-	-	M*	-	-	G	-	M*	D	-	D	-	-	D	-
v	r	-	te	-	-	r	-	hen	-	-	ge	-	-	ke	-
N	D	-	D	-	-	M*	-	M*	G	-	G	-	-	R	-
dil	-	-	bn	-	-	ke	-	dil	-	-	me	-	-	dh	-

|M* M* - M* | - - G - |G - - G | - -
d k - te | - - r - |hen - - ge | - -
interlude: flute:
R' R' R' R' R'M*' M*'-   G'- G'R'- R' R'-
R' R'M*' M*' G'- G'R'- R' R'-
R' R' M*'- G'M*'- G'M*'-
M*' M*'D' D' P'- P'M*'- M*'G'-   M*' M*'D' D' P'- P'M*'- M*'G'-
D'P'M*'G'-
synthe: R'- R'G' R'N R'N R' D-   R'N R'N R' D R'-

  R'R'   R'   R'R'   R'G'   R'R'   R'NR'R'D
(agr   mr gya   ruh   aaya   kare-gi-

DR'   R'R'   R' R'G'   R'N   DR'R'
tujhe dekh kr git   gaya karegi) -2

G'G'   R'N R' R' R' R'N DND
mujhe dekh kr tum n aansu bahana

D NDM* GM*GR R M* M*GGG
bs itni   gujarish hai tum muskurana

GG M*G G   M*G GM*   GM*DD
tere pyar men rng bhrte rhen-ge

D N D M* M*G G
ke dil bnke   dil me ...

44. TUM NE PUKARA AUR HAM

Film: Rajkumar (1964)
Lyrics: Shailendra
Taal: Kaharwa

Music: Shanker Jaikishan
Singer: Md. Rafi, Suman K.
Chord: PNR' RM*D RMD
S=C#

R: tum ne pukaaraa aaur hum chale aaye
      dil hathelee par le aaye re
S: tum ne pukaaraa aaur hum chale aaye
      jaan hathelee par le aaye re

R: aao baithho humaare pahaloo mein panaah le lo
      meree jalatee huyee aakhon pe ye aankhe rakh do
      aye mere pyaar ke khwaabon kee hasiin shahajaadi
      honthh kyo kaanp rahe hai, zaraa kuchh to bolo
R: tum ne pukaaraa aaur hum chale aaye
      jaan hathelee par le aaye re
S: aaj khelo meree zulfon se, ijaazat hai tumhe
      muz ko chhoo lo, meri nas nas mein sharaare bhar do
      mere diladaar, meri aakhon mein rahane waale
      mai tumhaari hoo, meri maang mein taare bhar do
R: tum ne pukaaraa aaur hum chale aaye
      dil hathelee par le aaye re

R: naam raushan hain tum hee se mere afasaane kaa
      zindagee naam hai ulafat mein jiye jaane kaa
      tum agar hum ko na milate to ye soorat hoti
      log le jaate janaazaa tere diwaane kaa
S: tum ne pukaaraa aaur hum chale aaye
      jaan hathelee par le aaye re

Vinod Kumar

TUM NE PUKARA AUR HAM

dha	ge	n	ti	n	ke	dhi	n	dha	ge	n	ti	n	ke	dhi	n
1	2	3	4	5	6	7	8	1	2	3	4	5	6	7	8
prelude:															
R'-------		S'	R'	G'	---------			R'------							
aa-------aa		aa	aa	------				aa -----							
music: P'M'G'R'S'N G'R'S'NDP				R' S' G' ----				S' N P ---							
										R	-	-	M*	-	P
										tum	-	-	ne	-	pu
D	-	D	-	D	-	D	-	-	-	N	S'	-	N	D	-
ka	-	ra	-	au	-	r	-	-	-	hm	-	-	ch	le	-
P	-	P	-	-	-	-	-	-	-	R'	-	-	-	N	-
aa	-	ye	-	-	-	-	-	-	-	dil	-	-	-	h	-
S'	-	S'	-	N	-	D	-	P	-	D	S'	N	-	-	-
the	-	li	-	p	r	le	-	aa	-	ye	-	re	-	-	-
S'	-	-	-	N	D	P	-	-	-	R	-	-	M*	-	P
-	-	-	-	-	-	-	-	-	-	tum	-	-	ne	-	pu
D	-	D	-	D	-	D	-	-	-	N	S'	-	N	D	-
ka	-	ra	-	au	-	r	-	-	-	hm	-	-	ch	le	-
P	-	P	-	-	-	-	-	-	-	R'	-	-	-	N	-
aa	-	ye	-	-	-	-	-	-	-	jan	-	-	-	h	-
S'	-	S'	-	N	-	D	-	P	-	D	S'	N	-	-	-
the	-	li	-	p	r	le	-	aa	-	ye	-	re	-	-	-
S'	-	-	-	N	D	P	-	-	-	R	-	-	M*	-	P
-	-	-	-	-	-	-	-	-	-	tum	-	-	ne	-	pu

D	-	D	-	D	-	D	-	-	-	N̠	S'	-	N̠	D	-
ka	-	ra	-	au	-	r	-	-	-	hm	-	-	ch	le	-

P	-	P	-	-	-	-	-	-	-
aa	-	ye	-	-	-	-	-	-	-

interlude:saxophone

S' R' ---- S' G̠' ---- G̠' R' ---- x2

R D ---- P N̠   D P---

synthe: D'P' P'M' M'G̠' G̠'R' M'—G̠' R' M'--- G̠' R' R'—

R'S' S'N̠ N̠D DP PDN̠—D P N̠ D P P-- R G̠ M P

MM   MP PMM   MPP P   MMP P   P
aao baitho hmare phlu me pnah le lo

DD   DD DD   DN̠   D   P   MP   P   P
meri jlti huii aankhon pe ye aankhe rkh do

S'   S'S'   S'S' S'   S'R'   S' N̠DP   N̠ N̠N̠
ae   mere   pyar ke khwabo ki hnsi- shahzadi

R'R' S'R' G̠'R' S'N̠S'   R'   DP MM   MP PP
hoth kyu kanp rhe-   hain, zra kuchh to- bolo

45. TUM SE O HASEENA KABHI

Film: Farz (1967)
Lyrics: Anand Bakshi
Taal: Kaharwa

Music: Laxmikant Pyarelal
Singer: Md. Rafi, Suman K.
Chord: PNR'   S=C

tumse o haseena kabhi mohabbat na maine karni thi -2
magar mere dil ne mujhe dhokha de diya -2

tumse o deewane kabhi mohabbat na maine karni thi -2
magar mere dil ne mujhe dhokha de diya -2

aag sulag gayi nas nas mein neend rahi na raha chain bas mein
todi jaaye na ab mujhse pyaar ki ye rasmein kasmein
a gayi bulbul kafas mein
tauba meri tauba ye apni haalat na maine karni thi -2
magar mere dil ne mujhe dhokha de diya ha-2

log ye mujhko hain samjhaate beet rahi thi hanste gaate
maine tumhein kisaliye chheda raahon mein aate jaate
mujhe sab hain sataate
tauba meri tauba ke ye sharaarat na maine karni thi -2
magar mere dil ne mujhe dhokha de diya ha -2

shaam savere dil ghabraaye
raaz e dil na khul jaaye
raat hamaare sapanon mein chhup ke
roz koi aaye jaaye kaahe neha lagaaye
tauba meri tauba ke ye qayaamat na maine karni thi -2
magar mere dil ne mujhe dhokha de diya ha -2

TUM SE O HASEENA KABHI

dha	-	-	ti	na	-	ghe	na	dha	-	-	ti	na	-	ghe	na
1	2	3	4	5	6	7	8	1	2	3	4	5	6	7	8

prelude:

RR PP x 8

R'R' P'P' M'M' G'G' R'R' S'S' NN DD

P- D- P- D- P- D- P-

R'R'R' M' R'R'R' M' R'R'R' M' R'R'R' M'

S'S'S'G'- NNNR'- DDDS'- PPPN-

PPPD x 4 P-

R- P- RPN- x 3 R- P-P-P- R- P- RPN- x 3 R- P-P-P-

		R'	-	N	N	-	N	N	-	R'	-	N	N	-	N
		tum	-	se	o	-	h	sii	-	na	-	k	bhi	-	mo
N	-	R'	-	N	N	-	N	N	D	D	N	N	-	D	-
ho	-	bt	-	na	main	-	ne	k	r	ni	-	thi	-	-	-
-	-	D	D	-	D	D	-	D	-	N̲	-	-	D	P	-
-	-	m	gr	-	me	re	-	dil	-	ne	-	-	mu	jhe	-
P	-	N	-	-	D	-	P	P	-	-	-	-	-	D	-
dho	-	kha	-	-	de	-	di	ya	-	-	-	-	-	aa	-
		R'	-	N	N	-	N	N	-	R'	-	N	N	-	N
-	-	tum	-	se	o	-	di	va	-	ne	-	k	bhi	-	mo
N	-	R'	-	N	N	-	N	N	D	D	N	N	-	D	-
ho	-	bt	-	na	main	-	ne	k	r	ni	-	thi	-	-	-
-	-	D	D	-	D	D	-	D	-	N̲	-	-	D	P	-
-	-	m	gr	-	me	re	-	dil	-	ne	-	-	mu	jhe	-
P	-	N	-	-	D	-	P	P	-	-	-	-	-	D	-
dho	-	kha	-	-	de	-	di	ya	-	-	-	-	-	ha	-

interlude: play sthayi and then play

P'- D'- R'G'- P'- D'- R'G'-

P- D- NR' PN x 4 NR'P

P- D- NR' PN x 4 NR'P

S'- S'R'S'NDN---

		N	R'	N	-	P	-	P	-	D	-	N	-	S'	-
		aa	-	-	-g	su	-	l	-	g	-	g	-	yi	-
R'	-	S'	-	S'	-	R'	-	R'	-	S'	-	-	-	-	-
n	-	s	-	n	-	s	-	me	-	-	-	-	-	-	-
-	-	ᴰN	-	-	-	M*	-	M*	-	P	-	D	-	N	-
-	-	nin	-	-	-d	r	-	hi	-	n	-	r	-	ha	-
N	-	-	-	S'	-	N	-	N	-	-	-	D	-	-	-
chai	-	-	-n	b	-	s	-	me	-	-	-	-	-	-	-
-	-	N	S'	N	-	P	-	P	-	D	-	N	-	S'	-
-	-	to	-	di	-	ja	-	ye	-	-	-	na	-	-	-
R'	-	S'	-	S'	-	S'	-	R'	-	S'	-	-	-	-	-
a	-	b	-	mu	-	jh	-	se	-	-	-	-	-	-	-
-	-	N	-	-	-	M*	-	M*	-	P	-	D	-	N	-
-	-	pya	-	-	-	r	-	ki	-	-	-	r	-	s	-
N	-	D	-	S'	-	N	-	N	-	-	-	N	-	N	-
me	-	-	-	k	-	s	-	me	-	-	-	aa	-	g	yi
D	-	-	D	-	-	P	-	P	-	P	-	P	-	-	-
bul	-	-	bul	-	-	k	-	f	-	s	-	me	-	-	-
-	-	R'	-	N	N	-	N	N	-	R'	-	N	N	-	N
-	-	tau	-	ba	me	-	ri	tau	-	ba	-	ye	a	p	ni

N	-	R'	-	N	N	-	N	N	D	D	N	N	-	D	-
ha	-	l	t	n	main	-	ne	k	r	ni	-	thi	-	-	-

-	-	D	D	-	D	D	-	D	-	N̲	-	-	D	P	-
-	-	m	gr	-	me	re	-	dil	-	ne	-	-	mu	jhe	-

P	-	N	-	-	D	-	P	P	-	-	-	-	-	D	-
dho	-	kha	-	-	de	-	di	ya	-	-	-	-	-	ha	-

interlude:

DP x 8 PDGMDNPDNS'DN

N N S'R'R' NS'— D D NS'S' DN-

N N S'R'R' NS'— D D NS'S' DN-

		N	R'	N	-	P	-	P	P	-	D		-	N	-
-	-	lo	-	-	-g	ye	-	mu	jh	-	ko	-	-	hain	-

R'	-	S'	-	S'	-	-	-	R'	-	S'	-	-	-	-	-
s	-	m	-	jha	-	-	-	te	-	-	-	-	-	-	-

-	-	N	-	-	-	M*	-	M*	-	P	-	D	-	N	-
-	-	bi	-	-	-t	r	-	hi	-	thi	-	hn	-	s	-

N	-	D	-	S'	-	N	-	N	-	-	-	-	-	-	-
te	-	-	-	ga	-	-	-	te	-	-	-	-	-	-	-

-	-	N	-	N	-	P	-	P	-	D	-	N	-	S'	-
-	-	main	-	ne	-	tu	-	mhe	-	-	-	kis	-	li	-

R'	-	S'	-	S'	-	-	-	R'	-	S'	-	-	-	-	-
ye	-	-	-	chhe	-	-	-	da	-	-	-	-	-	-	-

-	-	D	N	-	-	M*	-	M*	-	P	-	D	-	N	-
-	-	ra	-	-	-	ho	-	me	-	-	-	aa	-	-	-

N	-	D	-	S'	-	N	-	N	-	-	-	N	-	N	-
te	-	-	-	ja	-	-	-	te	-	-	-	mu	-	jhe	-

| N | D | - | D | - | - | P | - | P | - | - | - | P | - | - | - |
| s | b | - | hain | - | - | s | - | ta | - | - | - | te | - | - | - |

| - | - | R' | - | N | N | - | N | N | - | R' | - | N | N | - | N |
| - | - | tau | - | ba | me | - | ri | tau | - | ba | - | ke | ye | - | sh |

| N | - | R' | - | N | N | - | N | N | D | D | N | N | - | D | - |
| ra | - | r | t | n | main | - | ne | k | r | ni | - | thi | - | - | - |

| - | - | D | D | - | D | D | - | D | - | <u>N</u> | - | - | D | P | - |
| - | - | m | gr | - | me | re | - | dil | - | ne | - | - | mu jhe | - |

| P | - | N | - | - | D | - | P | P | - | - | - | - | - | D | - |
| dho | - | kha | - | - | de | - | di | ya | - | - | - | - | - | ha | - |

interlude:

RRP- RGM- MMD- MM

P D P D P S'NDP P D P D P S'NDP

P D P D G DNMP DNMP DNMP P-

NR'N   PPD   NS' R'S'S' R'S'   ᴰN M* M*P D ND S'N
sha-m svere dil ghbra- ye--, raz e dil na khul jae

NS'N PPD   NS'R' S' S'S' R'S' N   M*M*P DNND S'N
ra-t   hmare spno me chhup ke-, roz koii-   aa-ye- jae

NN   DD   PPP
kaahe neha lgaye

R'N   NN   NR' N N NN R' N   NN   NDDN ND
tauba meri tauba ke ye, qyamt n   mainne krni-   thi- -2

DD   DD   D <u>N</u> DP   PN   D PP   D
mgr mere dil ne mujhe dhokha de diya ha -2

46.   TUMHI MERE MEET HO

Film: Pyase Panchhi (1961)   Music: Kalyanji Anandji
Lyrics: Qamar Jalalabadi   Singer: Suman K. , Hemant Kumar
Taal: Kaharwa   Chord: GPN   S=C

S: tumhi mere meet ho tumhi meri priit ho -2
        tumhi meri aarzu ka pahala pahala giit ho
H: tumhi mere meet ho tumhi meri prit ho -2
        tumhi meri zindagi ki pahali pahali jiit ho
        tumhi mere meet ho

S: tum ho bechain sainya ham beqaraar se
        jaane naa dungi tumko naino ke dwaar se -2
H: teri nigaaho ne dekha hai pyaar se
        mila aaj pyaasa panchhi nadiya ki dhaar se
S: tumhi chitchor mere tumhi dil ki jiit ho -2
        tumhi meri aarzu ka pahela pahela giit ho
B: tumhi mere miit ho.

H: tu kisi baagbaan ke gulshan kaa phool hai
        chhup chhup ke tujhko chaaha rahi ki bhool hai
S: aa... rahi ki bhool nahi qismat ki bhool hai
        qismat ki bhool sainya hamko kubul hai
H: mere dil ke saaj ka tumhi tumhi sangiit ho -2
        tumhi meri zindagi ki pahali pahali jiit ho
B: tumhi mere meet ho tumhi meri priit ho
        tumhi meri zindagi ki pahali pahali jiit ho
        tumhi mere meet ho.

TUMHI MERE MEET HO

dha	ge	n	ti	n	ke	dhi	n	dha	ge	n	ti	n	ke	dhi	n
1	2	3	4	5	6	7	8	1	2	3	4	5	6	7	8

G'M*' G'P' G'M*' G'P' R'G' S'S' NS' N
aa-------------- tumhi mere mit ho
prelude:
    D P G R S R- M*- D P G R S R- G-
M* G M* G M* R S R- M*- D P G R S R- G-

1	2	3	4	5	6	7	8	1	2	3	4	5	6	7	8
								N	N	-	N	-	N		
								tu	mhi	-	me	-	re		
N	-	-	N	N	-	-	-	-	-	N	S'	-	D	-	D
mi	-	-	t	ho	-	-	-	-	-	tu	mhi	-	me	-	ri
D	-	-	D	D	-	-	-	-	-	P	P	-	P	-	M*
pri	-	-	t	ho	-	-	-	-	-	tu	mhi	-	me	-	ri
P	-	-	D	N	-	D	-	-	-	P	D	P	M*	P	M*
aa	-	-	r	zu	-	ka	-	-	-	p	h	la	p	h	la
G	-	-	G	G	-	-	-	-	-	N	N	-	N	-	N
gi	-	-	t	ho	-	-	-	-	-	tu	mhi	-	me	-	re
N	-	-	N	N	-	-	-	-	-	N	S'	-	D	-	D
mi	-	-	t	ho	-	-	-	-	-	tu	mhi	-	me	-	ri
D	-	-	D	D	-	-	-	-	-	P	P	-	P	-	M*
pri	-	-	t	ho	-	-	-	-	-	tu	mhi	-	me	-	ri
P	-	-	D	N	-	D	-	-	-	P	D	P	M*	P	M*
zin	-	-	d	gi	-	ki	-	-	-	p	h	li	p	h	li
G	-	-	G	G	-	-	-	-	-	N	N	-	N	-	N
ji	-	-	t	ho	-	-	-	-	-	tu	mhi	-	me	-	re

```
N    -    -    R' | S'   -    N    -  | -    -  |              |
mi   -    -    t  | ho   -    o    -  | -    -  |              |

interlude: GP – S'– N–  P– R'S'N–
           R'– S' ND DP PM*–
           M*'----G'R'S'NDPM*G--

                  |                  |  N    S'  | -   G'   -   G'
                  |                  |  tu   m   | -   ho   -   be

G'   -    -    G' | M*'  -    G'   -  | -    -    G'   M*' | -   R'   -   R'
chai -    -    n  | sai  -    ya   -  | -    -    hm   -   | -   be   -   q

R'   -    -    R' | R'   -    -    -  | -    -    S'   -   | S'  -    S'  -
ra   -    -    r  | se   -    -    -  | -    -    ja   -   | ne  -    na  -

N    S'   S'   -  | N    S'   S'   -  | -    -    R'   G'  | -   S'   -   N
dun  -    gi   -  | tu   m    ko   -  | -    -    nai  -   | -   no   -   ke

N    -    -    N  | N    -    -    -  | -    -    N    S'  | -   G'   -   G'
dwa  -    -    r  | se   -    -    -  | -    -    te   -   | -   ri   -   ni

G'   -    -    -  | M*'  -    G'   -  | -    -    G'   M*' | -   R'   -   R'
ga   -    -    -  | ho   -    ne   -  | -    -    de   -   | -   kha  -   hai

R'   -    -    R' | R'   -    -    -  | -    -    S'   S'  | -   S'   -   S'
pya  -    -    r  | se   -    -    -  | -    -    mi   la  | -   aa   -   j

N    -    S'   -  | N    -    S'   -  | -    -    S'   R'  | -   S'   -   N
pya  -    sa   -  | pn   -    chhi -  | -    -    n    di  | -   ya   -   ki

N    -    -    N  | N    -    P    -  | G    -    N    N   | -   N    -   N
dha  -    -    r  | se   -    -    -  | -    -    tu   mhi | -   chi  -   t

N    -    -    N  | N    -    N    -  | -    -    N    S'  | -   D    -   D
cho  -    -    r  | me   -    re   -  | -    -    tu   mhi | -   di   -   l
```

```
D    -    -    D  | D    -    -    -  | -    -    P    P  | -    P    -    M*
ji   -    -    t  | ho   -    -    -  | -    -    tu   mhi| -    me   -    ri

P    -    -    D  | N    -    D    -  | -    -    P    D  | P    M*   P    M*
aa   -    -    r  | zu   -    ka   -  | -    -    p    h  | la   p    h    la

G    -    -    G  | G    -    -    -  | -    -    N    N  | -    N    -    N
gi   -    -    t  | ho   -    -    -  | -    -    tu   mhi| -    me   -    re

N    -    -    R' | S'   -    N    -  | -    -
mi   -    -    t  | ho   -    o    -  | -    -
```

```
          NS'  G' G'  G' G' M*'G'  G'M*'R'-  R'  R' R'  R'
hemant:tu-  kisii  bagba  ki  gulshn  ka  ful  hai

     S'   S'   S'  NS'S'   N-S'    R'G'-S' N   NN   N
chhupchhup ke tujhko chha-ha ra--hi  ki  bhul hai

     M*'   G'   NS'G'  G' G'G'  M*'G'  G'M*'  R'   R'  R'R'R'
suman:aa.. aa... ra-hi  ki bhul nhin  kismt  ki bhul hai

     S'  S'   S'  NS'S'  NS'S'   S' R' S' NNN    N  P  G
kismt  ki  bhu-l sai-ya  hme to qubul  hai o—

     NN    N   N   NN  N   N S'  DDDD  D  -
hemant:mere dil  ke  saj  ka  tumhi sn-git  ho -2

     PP     PM*  P D N   D  PDP  M*PM*   GG   G
tumhi meri  zindgi  ki  phli  phli       jit   ho
```

47.   VO DEKHO DEKH RAHA THA PAPIHA

Film: Fariyad (1964)
Lyrics: Kedar Sharma
Taal: Kaharwa

Music: Snehal Bhaatkar
Singer: Mahendra Kumar,
Suman K.
Chord: GPS' S=C#

wo dekho dekha dekh raha tha papiha

papiha dekho dekh raha tha papiha

papiha jaake sabase kahega papiha

papiha bhala chup kyon rahega papiha

papiha dekho dekha dekh raha

rim jhim jhim badariya barase

aise men jaiyo nahin ghar se

hamra jiya ghabraaye

aji tum bin raha na jaae

sar sar sar chale sard hawaaen

ful hanse kaliyaan muskaae

hamko ye samajhaaye

ham milkar naachein gaayein

tim tim tim karate hain sitaare

ap hue hai jab se hamaare

ham fuule nahin samaaein

ham ghadi ghadi muskaaein

VO DEKHO DEKH RAHA THA PAPIHA

dha	ge	n	ti	n	ke	dhi	n	dha	ge	n	ti	n	ke	dhi	n
1	2	3	4	5	6	7	8	1	2	3	4	5	6	7	8

prelude:

D D D PDS'D P- G- GPDP G- R- RGP RGPG D-
D D D PDS'D P- G- GPDP G- R- RGP
PG R- G- G'- R'- S'-
PD G'- R'- S'- P- G'- S'-

1	2	3	4	5	6	7	8	1	2	3	4	5	6	7	8
											S'	D	S'	P	D
											vo	de	kho	de	kha
G'	-	R'	G'	S'	-	S'	R'	D	D	-	S'	D	S'	P	D
de	-	kh	r	ha	-	tha	p	pi	ha	-	p	pi	ha	de	kho
G'	-	R'	G'	S'	-	S'	R'	D	D	-	S'	D	S'	P	D
de	-	kh	r	ha	-	tha	p	pi	ha	-	p	pi	ha	ja	ke
G'	G'	R'	G'	S'	-	S'	R'	D	D	-	S'	D	S'	P	D
s	b	se	k	he	-	ga	p	pi	ha	-	p	pi	ha	bh	la
G'	G'	R'	G'	S'	-	S'	R'	D	D	-	S'	D	S'	P	D
chu	p	kyu	r	he	-	ga	p	pi	ha	-	p	pi	ha	de	kho
G'	-	R'	G'	S'	-	-	R'	D	-	-	-	-	-	-	-
de	-	kh	r	ha	-	-	-	tha	-	-	-	-	-	-	-
S'	-	G'	-	S'	-	-	S'	S'	S'	N	D	N	N	P	-
rim	-	jhim	-	jhim	-	-	b	d	ri	ya	-	b	r	se	-
D	-	G'	-	S'	-	S'	-	S'	-	N	D	N	N	P	-
ae	-	se	-	me	-	ja	i	yo	-	n	hin	gh	r	se	-
P	P	P	-	D	D	R'	R'	S'	-	-	N	-	-	D	P
h	m	ro	-	ji	ya	gh	b	ra	-	-	y	-	-	a	ji

P	P	P	-	D	N	-	R'	S'	-	-	S'	-	-	-	-
tu	m	bi	n	r	ha	-	n	ja	-	-	y	-	-	-	-

S'	-	G'	-	S'	-	S'	S'	S'	-	N	D	N	-	P	-
s	r	s	r	s	r	ch	le	s	r	d	h	va	-	yen	-

D	-	G'	G'	S'	-	S'	S'	S'	-	N	D	N	-	P	-
fu	-	l	hn	se	-	k	li	ya	-	mu	s	ka	-	yen	-

P	P	P	-	D	-	R'	R'	S'	-	-	-	N	-	D	P
h	m	ko	-	ye	-	s	m	jha	-	-	-	yen	-	h	m

P	P	P	-	D	-	R'	-	S'	-	-	-	S'	-	-	-
mi	l	k	r	na	-	chen	-	ga	-	-	-	yen	-	-	-

S'	G'	S'	S'S'S'	N	DNP		
tim	tim	tim	krte	hain	sitare,		

D	G'	G'S'	S'	S'S'	N	DNP
aap	hue	hain	jb	se	hmare	-2

PP	PP	DN	R'S'	N
hm	fule	nhin	sma	e,

DP	PP	PD	R'R'S'	S'
hm	ghdi	ghdi	muska	yen

48.   VO PARI KAHAAN SE LAAUN

Film: Pahchan (1970)   Music: Shanker Jaikishan
Lyrics: Verma Malik   Singer: Mukesh, Suman K.
Taal: Kaharwa   Chord: RM*N   S=C#

S: (vo pari kahaan se laaun teri dulhan jise banaaun
       ki gori koi pasand na aaye tujhako
       ki chhori koi pasand na aaye tujhako) -3

S: ye to meri hai saheli, dilavaali alabeli
       jaise motiyaa chameli, jaise pyaar ki paheli
       solah saal ki umar, kokaa-kolaa si kamar
       ratti bhar bhi qasar kahi aaye na nazar
       kuchh huaa hai asar?
M: gol jude me ye veni, aur veni me ye tahani
       kaise judiyo se ped ugaaye
       ye gagaaraam ke samajh me na aaye -2
S: vo pari kahaan se laaun teri dulhan jise banaaun
       ki gori koi pasand na aaye tujhako
       ki chhori koi pasand na aaye tujhako

S: aankh jisaki hai billi naam iskaa hai lilli
       aise kajare ki dhaar, jaise tikhi talavaar
       dekh hotho kaa ye rang dekh chalane kaa dhang
       kate angrezi baal, baandhaa reshami rumaal
       bolo kyaa hai khayaal?
M: ise jab liyaa taq meraa rang huaa faq
       chhori ho ke hajaamat karaaye
       ye gagaaraam ke samajh me na aaye
S: vo pari kahaan se laaun teri dulhan jise banaaun
       ki gori koi pasand na aaye tujhako

ki chhori koi pasand na aaye tujhako

S: nam iska kamal jaise ganne ki fasal
jaise khila hai gulab dekh phura hai panjab
dekh rup ki umang jaise hirni ka ang
jaise milti ho khajur aisa mukhde pe nur
bol hai manzur?

M: ye to nache chham chham mera nikale hai dam
ise bhangda kon nachaye?
ye gagaaraam ke samajh me na aaye

S: vo pari kahaan se laaun teri dulhan jise banaaun
ki gori koi pasand na aaye tujhako
ki chhori koi pasand na aaye tujhako

S: ye to sindh se hai aayi kare bee ae ki padhaayi
tang kurta paijama ye to chhokari hangama
jaise titli ke ang jaise udti patang
jaise koyal ki ku jaise khile khushbu
kahti hai i love u

M: he prabhu he prabhu tu hi tu tu hi tu
aise nakhare kaun uthaaye?
ye gagaaraam ke samajh me na aaye

S: vo pari kahaan se laaun teri dulhan jise banaaun
ki gori koi pasand na aaye tujhako
ki chhori koi pasand na aaye tujhako

S: na ye dil ki hai chhoti na ye pyar ki hai khoti
zara ho gayi hai moti tabhi lagti hai chhoti
dekh iske masal ghi khati hai asal
tere kheton me jaye tere hal bhi chalaaye
tere bade kam aaye

M: mujhe karo na hairan ye to lage pahalvan

ise kasarat kon karaye?

ye gagaaraam ke samajh me na aaye

S: vo pari kahaan se laaun teri dulhan jise banaaun

ki gori koi pasand na aaye tujhako

ki chhori koi pasand na aaye tujhako

S: chhodo ye to hai naadaan, kare sabko hairaan

nahin samjhega pyar bilkul hai ganwar

ise rahne do kanwara firne do mara mara

aao ham sab jaayein maza isko chakhaayein

hosh iske udaayein

M: ye hont jab khole baar baar yahi bole

gangaraam ki samajh mein n aaye

ye gangaraam ki samajh mein n aaye

VO PARI KAHAAN SE LAAUN

dha	ge	n	ti	n	ke	dhi	n	dha	ge	n	ti	n	ke	dhi	n
1	2	3	4	5	6	7	8	1	2	3	4	5	6	7	8

prelude:

NNNN NNNN DDDD DDDD

PPPP PPPP M*M*M*M* M*M*M*M*

NR'S'NDPM*GM*-

     N NR' R'R' S'ND DD DS'S' ND PDP

suman: vo pri kha se laun teri dulhn jise bnaun

   M* GM* GR RR P P- PM*M*

ki gori koii psnd n aaye tujhko

   M* GM* GR RR D DP PM*M*

ki chhori koii psnd n aaye tujhko

interlude: M* R' R' R'R' R'R' R'R' R'R' R'R'
          M* R' N NN NN NN NN NN
          M*M*PD M*R'ND M*M*PD M*R'ND
          NN NN NN NN R' N D P M*

        M* M M*M* M* MM*M* M*MM*M* M*MM*M*
suman: ye to meri hai sheli,   dilvali   albeli

        M*M* PPP   M*PP M*M* P-   P M*PP
jaise motiya chmeli, jaise   pyar ki pheli

        PM* P- P M*P   PM* PP   P M*P
solh sal ki umr, koka-kola sii kmr

        M*D D D DD DR'   R'   N NN
rtti bhr bhi qsr khin aaye n nzr

        Play Chord (RM*N)
        kuchh huaa hai asr?

        R'   R'R'   R' R' R'R'   R'   R'R' R' R' R'R'
mukesh: gol jude me ye veni, aur veni me ye tahni

        R'R'   NR'R'   R' R'S'S' NND
kaise judiyon se pe-d   ugaye

        D DDDS'   S' NND D P PM*
ye gngaram ki smjh me n aaye

        N NR' R'R' S' ND
suman: vo pri kaha se laun ...

play rest of the song as above.

49. YUN HI DIL NE CHAHA THA

Film: Dil Hi To Hai (1963)   Music: Raushan
Lyrics: Sahir Ludhiyanvi   Singer: Suman K.
Taal: Kaharwa   Chord: SM$\underline{D}$ S=C#

yunhi dil ne chaahaa thaa ronaa rulaanaa
teri yaad to ban gayi ik bahaanaa

hame bhi nahi ilm, ham jis pe roye
vo biti rute hai ke aataa zamaanaa
vo biti rute hai ke aataa zamaanaa
teri yaad to ban gayi ik bahaanaa

gam-e-dil bhi hai aur gam-e-zindagi bhi
na isakaa thikaanaa na usakaa thikaanaa
na isakaa thikaanaa na usakaa thikaanaa
teri yaad to ban gayi ik bahaanaa

koi kis pe tadape, koi kisape roye
idhar dil jalaa hai, udhar aashiyaanaa
idhar dil jalaa hai, udhar aashiyaanaa
teri yaad to ban gayi ik bahaanaa

yunhi dil ne chaahaa thaa ronaa rulaanaa
teri yaad to ban gayi ik bahaanaa

YUN HI DIL NE CHAHA THA

dha	ge	n	ti	n	ke	dhi	n	dha	ge	n	ti	n	ke	dhi	n
1	2	3	4	5	6	7	8	1	2	3	4	5	6	7	8
prelude: sitar: G̲ D̲ P D̲ M															
														M	-
														yu	-
P	-	G̲	-	-	M	-	P	N̲	-	-	-	N̲	-	N̲	-
hi	-	-	-	-	dil	-	ne	chha	-	-	-	ha	-	tha	-
-	-	N̲	S'	-	S'	-	N̲	N̲	-	-	-	D̲	-	P	-
-	-	ro	-	-	na	-	ru	la	-	-	-	na	-	-	-
M	-	M	M	-	M	-	M	M	P	-	-	M	-	G̲	-
-	-	te	ri	-	ya	-	d	to	-	-	-	bn	-	-	-
-	-	P	P	-	D̲	-	P	M	-	-	-	M	-		
-	-	g	yi	-	i	k	b	ha	-	-	-	na	-		

interlude:

Synthe: M G̲ M D̲ P D̲ S' N R' S' M' –

sitar: N̲ D̲ P N̲ S' R' – R' – N̲ D̲ D̲ N̲

flute: MD̲PMG̲ SMG̲D̲ MG̲ SMGM

dha	ge	n	ti	n	ke	dhi	n	dha	ge	n	ti	n	ke	dhi	n
1	2	3	4	5	6	7	8	1	2	3	4	5	6	7	8
														M	-
														h	-
P	N̲	D̲	N̲	-	P	-	M	M	-	-	-	M	-	M	-
me	-	-	-	-	bhi	-	n	hin	-	-	-	il	-	m	-
-	-	G	-	-	M	-	P	G	-	M	-	R	-	S	-
-	-	hm	-	-	Jls	-	pe	ro	-	-	-	ye	-	-	-
-	-	P	P	-	P	-	P	P	-	D̲	-	M	-	M	-
-	-	vo	bi	-	ti	-	ru	te	-	-	-	hain	-	ke	-
-	-	D	-	-	D	-	N̲	P	-	-	-	M	-	M	
-	-	aa	-	-	ta	-	z	ma	-	-	-	na	-	vo	-

| P | - | <u>G</u> | - | - | M | - | P | <u>N</u> | - | - | - | <u>N</u> | - | <u>N</u> | - |
| bi | - | - | - | - | ti | - | ru | te | - | - | - | hain | - | ke | - |

| - | - | <u>N</u> | S' | - | S' | - | <u>N</u> | <u>N</u> | - | - | - | <u>D</u> | - | P | - |
| - | - | aa | - | - | ta | - | z | ma | - | - | - | na | - | - | - |

| M | - | M | M | - | M | - | M | M | P | - | - | M | - | <u>G</u> | - |
| - | - | te | ri | - | ya | - | d | to | - | - | - | bn | - | - | - |

| - | - | P | P | - | <u>D</u> | - | P | M | - | - | - | M | - |
| - | - | g | yi | - | i | k | b | ha | - | - | - | na | - |

R' R'   S'   R' R'<u>N</u> <u>NN</u> R' R' S'R' R'<u>N</u> <u>N</u>-
gm e   dil bhi hai- aur gm e zindgi- bhi-

<u>N</u> <u>NN</u>M PS'S' S' <u>NN</u>M P<u>NN</u>
n iska thikana n uska thikana

M P<u>G</u>M P<u>NN</u>   <u>N</u> <u>N</u>S'S' <u>NN</u> DPM
n iska thikana n uska thikana—

MM MM MP M <u>G</u> PP <u>D</u> PMM
teri yad to- bn-- gayi ik bahana

MP<u>NDN</u> P M MMM GG M P MGM R S
koii   kis pe tdpe koii kis pe ro----ye—

PP   P P P<u>D</u> M DD D <u>N</u> P M
idhr dil jla-- hai udhr aashiyana

MP<u>G</u> M P<u>N</u> <u>N</u> <u>NN</u>S' S'<u>NN</u> <u>D</u>PM
idhr dil jla hai udhr aashiyana---

MM MM MP M <u>G</u> PP <u>D</u> PMM
teri yad to- bn-- gayi ik bahana

50.   YE KISNE GEET CHHEDA

Film: Meri Surat Teri Aankhein (1963)   Music: Sachindev Burman
Lyrics: Shailendra   Singer: Mukesh, Suman K.
Taal: Daadra   Chord: SGP   S=E

ye kisane giit chheda -2
dil mera naache, thirak, thirak, ye kisane giit chheda
ye kisaki zulf bikhari -2
jag saara gaya, mahak, mahak, ye kisaki zulf bikhari

chori chori, hole hole, thhndi thhndi, hawa aye -2
kaliyon ke, mukh chume, bagiya ko, dularaaye
daali daali, jaaye lachak lachak kisaki zulf bikhari
ye kisane giit chheda -2
dil mera naache, thirak, thirak, ye kisane giit chheda

tumane hi, kiya tona, tumane hi, jaadu fera
anjaani, dagari pe, chala dekho man mera
matawaala, gaya bahak bahak kisane giit chheda
ye kisaki zulf bikhari -2
jag saara gaya, mahak, mahak, ye kisaki zulf bikhari

ek baazi, maine jiti, ek baaji, dil haara -2
mere saajan, tere kaaran, maine chhoda, jag saara
sng tere chali runak jhunak kisane giit chheda
ye kisaki zulf bikhari -2
jag saara gaya, mahak, mahak, ye kisaki zulf bikhari
ye kisane giit chheda -2
dil mera naache, thirak, thirak, ye kisane giit chheda -2

YE KISNE GEET CHHEDA

dhi	na	ti	na	dhi	na	dhi	na	ti	na	dhi	na
1	2	3	4	5	6	1	2	3	4	5	6

prelude:
PDPMP -2 PDPMP -2 PS'   P- DPM
hu-------- aa------   aa--- aa------

flute: MP MGM -2 DPDMP-
guitar: G'R'S'ND PDN S'R'G' -2 P G P G' S'-

dhi	na	ti	na	dhi	na	dhi	na	ti	na	dhi	na
										S	-
										ye	-
R	G	S	R	.N	S	S	-	S	-	G	G
ki	s	ne	gi	-	t	chhe	-	da	-	di	l
G	M	-	-	G	R	G	R	S	R	S	.N
me	ra	-	-	na	che	thi	r	k	thi	r	k
S	G	S	R	.N	S	S	-	S	-	S	-
ki	s	ne	gi	-	t	chhe	-	da	-	ye	-
R	G	S	R	.N	S	S	S	S	-	G	G
ki	s	ki	zu	-	lf	bi	kh	ri	-	j	g
G	M	-	-	G	R	G	R	S	R	S	.N
sa	ra	-	-	g	ya	m	h	k	m	h	k
S	G	S	R	.N	S	S	S	S	-		
ki	s	ki	zu	-	lf	bi	kh	ri	-		

interlude: P—DS'D DS'DPG—GMP—D--- DP-

dhi	na	ti	na	dhi	na	dhi	na	ti	na	dhi	na
										G	G
										cho	ri
M	P	-	-	D	N	P	D	-	-	N	D
cho	ri	-	-	hau	le	hau	le	-	-	thn	di

D	P	M	-	P	D	P	P	-*	-	M	G
thn	di	-	-	h	va	aa	ye	-	-	k	li
M	P	-	-	D	N	D	D	-	-	N	D
yon	ke	-	-	mu	kh	chu	me	-	-	b	gi
D	P	M	-	P	D	P	P	G	P	G	G
ya	ko	-	-	du	l	ra	ye	-	-	da	li
G	M	-	-	G	R	G	R	S	R	S	.N
da	li	-	-	ja	ye	l	ch	k	l	ch	k
S	G	S	R	.N	S	S	S	S	-	S	-
ki	s	ki	zu	-	lf	bi	kh	ri	-	ye	-
R	G	S	R	.N	S	S	-	S	-	G	G
ki	s	ne	gi	-	t	chhe	-	da	-	di	l
G	M	-	-	G	R	G	R	S	R	S	.N
me	ra	-	-	na	che	thi	r	k	thi	r	k
S	G	S	R	.N	S	S	-	S	-		
ki	s	ne	gi	-	t	chhe	-	da	-		

interlude: PP PP P- GG GG G- GG GG G- S.N S G S-

										G	G
										tu	m
M	P	-	-	D	N	D	D	-	-	D	N
ne	hi	-	-	ki	ya	to	na	-	-	tu	m
D	P	M	-	P	D	P	P	-*	-	M	G
ne	hi	-	-	ja	du	fe	ra	-	-	a	n
M	P	-	-	D	N	D	D	-*	-	N	D
ja	ni	-	-	d	g	ri	pe	-	-	ch	la

D	P	M	-	P	D	P	P	G	P	G	G
de	kho	-	-	m	n	me	ra	-	-	m	t
G	M	-	-	G	R	G	R	S	R	S	.N
va	la	-	-	g	ya	b	h	k	b	h	k
S	G	S	R	.N	S	S	-	S	-	S	-
ki	s	ne	gi	-	t	chhe	-	da	-	ye	-
S	G	S	R	.N	S	S	S	S	-	G	G
ki	s	ki	zu	-	lf	bi	kh	ri	-	j	g
G	M	-	-	G	R	G	R	S	R	S	.N
sa	ra	-	-	g	ya	m	h	k	m	h	k
S	G	S	R	.N	S	S	S	S	-		
ki	s	ki	zu	-	lf	bi	kh	ri	-		

interlude: P—DS'D DS'DPG—GMP—D--- DP-interlude:

										G	G
										e	k
M	P	-	-	D	N	D	D	-	-	D	N
ba	zi	-	-	main	ne	ji	ti	-	-	e	k
D	P	M	-	P	D	P	P	-*	-	M	G
ba	zi	-	-	di	l	ha	ra	-	-	me	re
M	P	-	-	D	N	D	D	-	-	N	D
sa	jn	-	-	te	re	ka	rn	-	-	main	ne
D	P	M	-	P	D	P	P	G	P	G	G
chho	da	-	-	j	g	sa	ra	-	-	sn	g
G	M	-	-	G	R	G	R	S	R	S	.N
te	re	-	-	ch	li	ru	n	k	jhu	n	k

S	G	S	R	.N	S	S	-	S	-
ki	s	ne	gi	-	t	chhe	-	da	-

-* music: S' D S'--- P G P --- (for repeating the line)

51. YE MAUSAM RANGEEN SAMAA

Film: Modern Girl (1961)　　　　Music: Ravi
Lyrics: Gulshan Bawra　　　　Singer: Mukesh, Suman K.
Taal: Kaharwa　　　　Chord: SGP　S=B

ye mausam rangin sama, thahar zra o jaan-e-jaan
tera mera, mera tera pyaar hai, to fir kaisa sharamaana
ruk to main jaaun jaan-e-jaan, mujhako hai inkaar kahaan
tera mera, mera tera pyaar sanam na ban jaaye afsaana

ye chaand ye sitaare, kahate hain mil ke saare, aaja pyaar karein
ye chnda bairi dekhe, aise men bolo kaise iqraar karein
dil men hai kuchh, kuchh kahe zubaan pyaar yahi hai jaan-e-jaan
tera mera, mera tera pyaar hai, to fir kaisa sharamaana

ye pyar ki lambi rahen, kahati hain ye nigahen kahin dur chalein
baithe hain ghera daale, ye zaalim duniya waale, hamen dekh jale
jalata hai to jale jahaan thhahar jra o jaan-e-jaan
tera mera, mera tera pyaar sanam na ban jaaye afsaana

Vinod Kumar

YE MAUSAM RANGEEN SAMAA

dha	ge	n	ti	n	ke	dhi	n	dha	ge	n	ti	n	ke	dhi	n
1	2	3	4	5	6	7	8	1	2	3	4	5	6	7	8
S'	-	S'	N	S'	-	S'	N	S'	N	D	P	M	-	-	-
ye	-	mau	-	sm	-	rn	-	gi	-	n	s	ma	-	-	-
N	N	N	D	N	-	N	D	N	D	P	M	G	-	-	-
th	h	r	z	ra	-	o	-	ja	-	ne	-	ja	-	-	-
S	S	S	R	G	G	G	M	P	-	-	D	N	-	N	-
te	ra	me	ra	me	ra	te	ra	pya	-	-	r	hai	-	to	-
N	S'	S'	G'	R'	-	S'	S'	N	-	S'	-	-	-	-	-
fi	r	kai	-	sa	-	sh	r	ma	-	na	-	-	-	-	-

music: P- G'- R'- S'ND NR'S'

dha	ge	n	ti	n	ke	dhi	n	dha	ge	n	ti	n	ke	dhi	n
S'	-	S'	N	S'	-	S'	N	S'	N	D	P	M	-	-	-
ru	k	to	main	ja	-	un	-	ja	-	ne	-	ja	-	-	-
N	N	N	D	N	-	N	D	N	D	P	M	G	-	-	-
mu	jh	ko	-	hai	-	i	n	ka	-	r	k	ha	-	-	-
S	S	S	R	G	G	G	M	P	-	-	D	N	-	N	-
te	ra	me	ra	me	ra	te	ra	pya	-	r	s	nm	-	na	-
N	S'	S'	G'	R'	-	S'	S'	N	-	S'	-	-	-	-	-
b	n	ja	-	e	-	a	f	sa	-	na	-	-	-	-	-

interlude: P P D – PDPDPG P P D –
   P' P' D' – P'D'P'D'P'G' P' P' D'-
   G' --- P' --- G'P'G'R'S'- G' --- P' --- G' R' S'
   P P D PDPDPG PPD NR'G'-

															G'
															ye
G'	-G'	G'	G'	S'	D	-	G'	G'	G'	G'	G'	S'	D	D	R'
chan	-d	ye	si	ta	re	-	kh	te	hain	mil	ke	sa	re	aa	ja

S'	-	S'S'	S'	-	-	P	D	R'	-	-	S'	R'	S'	-	G'
pya	-	r,k	ren	-	-	-	-	-	-	-	-	-	-	-	ye

G'	-G'	G'	G'	S'	D	-	G'	G'	G'	G'	G'	S'	D	D	R'
chan	-d	ye	si	ta	re	-	kh	te	hain	mil	ke	sa	re	aa	ja

S'	-	S'S'	S'	-	-	-	G'	G'	-G'	G'	G'	S'	D	-	G'
pya	-	r,k	ren	-	-	-	ye	chn	da	bai	ri	de	khe	-	ae

G'	G'	G'	G'	S'	D	D	R'	S'	-S'	S'	S'	-	-	-	-
se	me	bo	lo	kai	se	i	q	ra	-r	k	ren	-	-	-	-

S'	-	S'	N	S'	-	S'	N	S'	N	D	P	M	-	-	-
di	l	me	hai	ku	chh	ku	chh	k	he	-	zu	ba	-	-	-

N	-	N	D	N	-	N	D	N	D	P	M	G	-	-	-
pya	-	r	y	hi	-	hai	-	ja	-	ne	-	ja	-	-	-

S	S	S	R	G	G	G	M	P	-	-	D	N	-	N	-
te	ra	me	ra	me	ra	te	ra	pya	-	-	r	hai	-	to	-

N	S'	S'	G'	R'	-	S'	S'	N	-	S'	-	-	-	-	-
fi	r	kai	-	sa	-	sh	r	ma	-	na	-	-	-	-	-

interlude: S' R' G' R' D – D N S' N P ---

       S' R' G' R' D – D N S' N P ---

       G'R'S'DP- ND R'S' G'R' P'G' D'P' S'R'G'-

G' G' G' G'G' S'D G'G' G' G' G'S'D DR' S'S' S'S'
ye pyar ki lmbi rahe kahti hain ye nigahe, khin dur chle

G'G' G' G'G' S'D G' G'G' G'G' S'D DR' S'S' S'S'
baithe hain ghera dale ye zalim duniya vale, hme dekh jle

S' S'N S' S'N S'ND PM NN DN ND NDPMG
jlata- hai to- jle- jhan, thhr zra o- ja-n-e-jan
tera mera ...

52. SARGAM OR ALANKAR OR PALTE

S R G M P D N S'
S' N D P M G R S

SS RR GG MM PP DD NN S'S'
S'S' NN DD PP MM GG RR SS

SSS RRR GGG MMM PPP DDD NNN S'S'S'
S'S'S' NNN DDD PPP MMM GGG RRR SSS

SR RG GM MP PD DN NS'
S'N ND DP PM MG GR RS

SRG- RGM- GMP- MPD PDN- DNS'-
S'ND- NDP- DPM- PMG- MGR- GRS-

SRGM RGMP GMPD MPDN PDNS'
S'NDP NDPM DPMG PMGR MGRS

SRGMP RGMPD GMPDN MPDNS'
S'NDPM NDPMG DPMGR PMGRS

SG RM GP MD PN DS'
S'D NP DM PG MR GS

SM RP GD MN PS'
S'P NM DG PR MS

SP RD GN MS'
S'M NG DR PS

SD RN GS'
S'G NR DS

SRSRG- RGRGM- GMGMP- MPMPD- PDPDN- DNDNS'-
S'NS'ND- NDNDP- DPDPM- PMPMG-MGMGR- GRGRS-

SRGSRSRG RGMRGRGM GMPGMGMP
MPDMPMP PDNPDPD DNS'DNDNS'

S'NDS'NS'ND NDPNDNDP DPMDPDPM
PMGPMPMG MGMGMGR GRSGRGRS

S
S R S
S R G R S
S R G M G R S
S R G M P M G R S
S R G M P D P M G R S
S R G M P D N D P M G R S
S R G M P D N S' S' N D P M G R S

S'
S' N S'
S' N D N S'
S' N D P D N S'
S' N D P M P D N S'
S' N D P M G M P D N S'
S' N D P M G R G M P D N S'
S' N D P M G R S R G M P D N S'

S-SRG- R-RGM- G-GMP- M-MPD- P-PDN- D-DNS'-
S'-S'ND- N-NDP- D-DPM- P-PMG- M-MGR- G-GRS-

RS GR MG PM DP ND S'N R'S'
NS' DN PD MP GM RG SR .NS

SGR RMG GPM MDP PND DS'N NR'S'
S'DN NPD DMP PGM MRG GSR R.NS

.P P .DD .NN SS' RR' GG' MM'
M'M G'G R'R S'S N.N D.D P.P

S <u>R</u> <u>G</u> M P <u>D</u> <u>N</u> S'
S' <u>N</u> <u>D</u> P M <u>G</u> <u>R</u> S

S <u>R</u> G M P <u>D</u> N S'
S' N <u>D</u> P M G <u>R</u> S

53.   Other books of Vinod Kumar

Mukesh 51 songs' sargam, Part-1, 2

Lata 51 songs' sargam

Kishore 51 songs' sargam, Part-1, 2

Md. Rafi 51 songs' sargam, Part-1,2,3,4

Asha 51 songs' sargam

SD Burman and Yesudas 51 songs' sargam

Manna Dey 51 songs' sargam

Kumar Shanu 51 songs' sargam

Composer SD Burman 51 songs' sargam

Suman Kalyanpur 51 songs' sargam

Superhit 51 Gazals sargam

Bhajan swarlipi, Part-1,2,3

Sloan Duployan Shorthand book

These Books are also available in English SRGM and Western CDEFG style at notionpress.com and amazon.in and at Flipkart.com

For English SRGM books search… (Singer name) 51 Songs' Sargam, book.

For Western CDEFG books search… (Singer name) Songs' Western Notes, book.

If you like the books, pl. tell others.

vinod kumar (vinod66vk@gmail.com)

Scan to Purchase from flipkart.com
Scan to Purchase from amazon.in
Enquiry may be made at mob: 9452904656
These books are available online only.

Scan below QR Code from your mobile to get Vinod Kumar's (Singer name) 51 Songs' Sargam books from Flipkart.com site . (Hindi, English, Western all)

Scan below QR Code from your mobile to get Vinod Kumar's (Singer name) 51 Songs' Sargam books from Amazon.in site . (Hindi, English, Western all)

ASHA
LATA
SUPERHIT 51 GAZALS'
S.D. Burman
KISHORE
KISHORE
KUMAR SHANU
MANNA DEY
MD RAFI
Md RAFI
MUKESH
MUKESH
Hindi सा रे ग म
English SRGM
And
Western CDEF
All type books